Don't Cry, Pappa

Surviving Persistent Depression and Heartbreaking Tragedies to Find a New Mission in Life

Gunnar E Skollingsberg PhD

ISBN: 1505426189
ISBN 13: 9781505426182
Library of Congress Control Number: 2014922473
CreateSpace Independent Publishing Platform
North Charleston, South Carolina

To the children...
May their lives be filled with laughter and joy – every day.

Contents

One

A New Beginning

Every child begins the world again.
—Henry David Thoreau

The antiseptic-laden air greeted me as I passed through the front doors of the hospital on that clear, warm day in May. The ancient, wrinkled woman at the front desk appeared agitated.

"Where have you been?" she snapped. "We've been looking for you!"

"What's the problem?" I asked, beginning to feel frightened.

I was then a young man, twenty-six years old, and I was about to be a father. We lived in a small town in southern Idaho, and I had brought my wife, Janet, into our community hospital very early that day when she started labor. We were both nervous and even somewhat scared of this new life experience that was rapidly approaching.

Unfortunately, we found out that morning that some of our fears were justified; there were complications. As the labor progressed, it was discovered that our baby was presenting breech; apparently, he didn't like being upside down. Our doctor told us that he was going to have to deliver the baby through Cesarean section. My wife was given medications to slow the contractions and delay the labor while they called in staff and made preparations.

"Don't worry," we were told. "Everything will be fine."

The operation was scheduled for later that afternoon. I had already been at the hospital for several hours, so it was suggested that I take a short break. I went home to quickly clean up, change my clothes, and grab a sandwich before returning to the hospital.

The old woman at the front desk scowled at me.

"I was told that the operation was scheduled for four o'clock," I said. "What happened?"

"Well, the baby didn't wait!" she barked.

It felt like a miracle occurred that day. Although this event has been repeated billions of times throughout the millions of years of human existence—and continues to be repeated thousands of times each day in every corner of the world—it was still a miracle to me: the bonding between parent and child, that permanent connection that gives meaning to life.

As I stood in the nursery hallway and looked through the large glass window at this newborn child—*my* child—I remember thinking, *This is amazing.* He was no longer just the bumps and kicks and movements that I had felt on my wife's extended abdomen; this was real—he was here! I then realized something else that was remarkable; my son was actually…*beautiful!*

In the past, I had often thought that newborn babies were, at best, somewhat funny-looking, and I had occasionally even held the opinion that some newborns were actually rather ugly. But here was *my* son, *my* child, with his wrinkled skin, misshapen head, wisps of dark hair, and puffy eyes. He was perfect.

This little miracle was apparently enjoying his newfound freedom, softly crying and jerking his little arms, flexing his tiny fingers, kicking his legs.

Amazing, I thought again.

For a long time, I just stood there, watching this little wonder—this new life. I thought about how my own world was now changed. Forever. I knew that, from this moment on, I was responsible for this new person. That was a frightening thought, but I was glad he was here. This beautiful baby was now my purpose in life—my reason for living.

I was going to take care of this precious little baby. I knew that I was now going to have to feed him, dress him, clean him, take care of him, and help him grow. I needed to teach him how to walk, talk, run, and play. It was my plan to help this baby grow up to be the best person he could be. It was an awesome responsibility, but I welcomed it. I wanted it. I *needed* it.

As I continued to watch him, my mind went far into the future, and I began to think, *How can I possibly ever let this boy go from me when he grows up to be a man, when he goes to college, and when he moves away?* I already knew that I would miss him terribly when that time came. But he had his own life to live, and I was there to love him and prepare him and give him the best start I could.

In that hospital corridor, an eternal bond formed between father and son.

I realized at that point that not only was my life now changed, *I* was changed—forever and completely. And, for the first time in my life, I really *knew* what love was, how it really felt. I knew I *loved* this beautiful baby boy.

"Erik," I whispered to him through the glass. This was the first time I had spoken his name aloud since his birth.

"Erik," I repeated. It sounded good. It fit.

Later, the doctor explained that Erik had come quickly, before the surgery could be set up. During the birth process, however, his umbilical cord had been pinched between his head and his mother's cervix, and thus his air supply had been interrupted for several minutes. Extra oxygen was given to him just after his birth, and the possibility of brain damage was disclosed.

At that time, I was a young special education teacher, so I had some knowledge and understanding of the possible dangers and problems associated with oxygen deprivation during the birth process. But this possibility didn't frighten me; I knew that—even if there were any problems—my son could (and would) still live a complete and fulfilling life. At that point, however, this was only a possibility; it was something I would watch for as Erik grew and developed. I loved this beautiful boy just the way he was.

Staring at the little, squirming wonder on the other side of the glass, I could hardly believe everything that had happened that day: the miracle of birth, of new life, and of becoming a parent.

It seemed that—possibly for the first time in my life—I was actually *happy!* What a remarkable feeling!

In that hospital corridor, I made a promise to my little boy. I promised my son that his life would be *much* better than the life I had lived—or rather, the life I had *endured*—up to that point. Erik would be loved, cared for, taught, and cherished (which were feelings that I had not experienced when I was a child). Erik would know that *he* was very much wanted and very much welcome.

Erik was my beautiful, precious baby boy.

Thus began a new chapter in my life, one that would—and did—bring me the love I had been missing and the happiness I had long sought. I later found, however, that this wonderful, miraculous event also exposed my life to the dark depths of unimaginable sorrows.

Two

My Early Childhood

Loneliness breaks the spirit.
—Jewish Proverb

There are many memories that remain in my mind from my
early childhood, most of which are negative. Among my
impressions of that time are feelings of being separate and different from those around me, and this fed a pervasive sense of
loneliness on my part. Even when I was surrounded by people,
I still felt utterly, almost desperately alone.

The source of my feeling of loneliness—this sense of separ-
ateness—was likely based on several factors. First, ours was an
immigrant family; we came to the United States from Norway.
At that time, our family consisted of father, mother, and three
sons. I was the youngest child, being just a few weeks old when
we arrived.

I'm certain my entire family experienced a strong sense of
isolation after we moved. Neither my parents nor my brothers
could read, write, or speak English. We were living in a new
country with different customs and different ways of doing
things.

As immigrants, there were many things we as a family did not know or understand: What were the accepted ways of speech and manners involved in social interactions in America? What behaviors were considered faux pas? What did we do that sometimes made people look at us so strangely? What caused them to laugh at us on occasion? It was a constant trial-and-error learning process. Even as a young child, I became keenly aware that we were not like the other families we encountered in our neighborhood or in our church.

As I grew up, I also had the personal sense of being different, of not being the same as others. One of the first things I became aware of was that our language was different. We spoke Norwegian at home, and I was learning English from other children in the neighborhood. With all these words from two different languages in my head, however, I often had problems keeping them separate; I wasn't always sure which words were English and which were Norwegian. When talking to my friends, I remember that they would sometimes give me a funny look after I said something. That's when I realized that they didn't understand me, so I would go over in my mind the words I had just used. I had to quickly decide which words were Norwegian and which were English. Then, I repeated my statement with some different words, hoping that I had changed the right ones. If a look of understanding came to my playmates' faces, then I knew that I was successful. If not, then I either tried again or gave up, saying, "Never mind."

Even our names constantly set us apart from others. Although these names were quite common in Norway, we found that they were sometimes objects of ridicule in the United States, especially when we were young. Whenever I was introduced to someone—or when I introduced myself—it would invariably lead to a two- or three-minute session of trying to get the other person to understand me or to pronounce my name. Often, they would pronounce it as "GOON-er" or "Gi-NAR," or sometimes my name would simply be transformed to "Gunther." It was not until I had attended college for a couple of years before I finally adopted the pronunciation of "Gunner" for my first name (which also occasionally produced raised eyebrows, comments, and chuckles itself). But at least this eliminated the complicated, painful repetition and pronunciation sessions. My brothers essentially changed their names, as well, but they did this at a younger age than I did. My oldest brother adopted a name that was just a distant approximation of his real name, and my other brother eventually had people call him by his first and middle name initials. I'm sure that my brothers also tired of explaining and pronouncing their "strange" names for others.

The foods we ate at home also made me feel different. Of course, my parents enjoyed the types of foods and meals they had grown up with (from the "old country"), and they naturally continued to try to maintain a somewhat similar diet in our new land. For example, our typical breakfast consisted of slices of bread with various toppings, such as cheese, fish, or meat. Occasionally, a soft-boiled egg might be added. This was fine and acceptable in our house, and this was normal for us and for me. But outside our home, when the subject of breakfasts came up, I learned that other people in America ate a variety of foods that might include eggs (prepared in various ways), bacon, sausages, or ham, toast, hash-brown potatoes, pancakes, waffles, hot chocolate, orange or tomato juice, and so on. I thought that Americans must certainly have such wonderful feasts for breakfast, while I just ate slices of bread.

I remember one day in elementary school, when we were having a nutrition lesson, the teacher asked each individual student to tell her—and the class—what we had eaten for breakfast that morning. When I realized what she was doing, I immediately felt mortified. There was *no* way that I was going to say, "Three slices of bread with goat cheese, sardines, and strawberry jam." Although that was the truth, this would have made me an object for ridicule from my classmates. Instead, while the teacher worked her way up and down the rows of desks, asking each student in turn to respond, I rehearsed in my mind what I thought would be a good, typical American breakfast. I repeated it to myself several times. When it came to my turn, I rattled off what I thought was a perfect breakfast: "Two fried eggs, bacon, hash browns, and a piece of toast." The smile and look on my teacher's face showed that she didn't believe me, but that was all right. I thought that I was at least safe from ridicule from my classmates—but I was wrong. Several students burst out in laughter. I didn't understand.

"A *piece* of toast?" one classmate shouted. "I wonder how big a piece he had!"

Another student held up his hand with his thumb and index finger about an inch apart, indication a very small piece. Then it seemed like the whole class laughed. Even with all my preparation, I had still used the wrong word; I had said *piece* when I should have said *slice*. I filed that fact away in my mind for future reference. But at that moment, I was embarrassed again, and I was once more reminded that I was different.

It wasn't until several years later that I realized that very few of my friends and classmates had breakfasts like we were shown and had discussed in school. Probably 90 percent of them ate a quick bowl of cold cereal in the morning! Hell, *they* were lying in class as well! But the damage had already been done; I had been identified as the odd one.

The lunches that I brought to school also set me apart from my classmates, and this continued even into my high school years. My sandwiches were made from homemade bread. I enjoyed my mother's bread, especially when it came hot out of the oven. But that was at home—not at school. Our homemade bread was about twice the size and almost double as thick as the sandwiches that were made from the store-bought bread that my classmates had. Even though my homemade bread tasted better than my classmates' bland, air-filled bread, it made me stand out as being different, and I felt that I was a target of ridicule and snickering every time I opened my lunch sack. I once asked my mother if we could have store-bought bread too (at least for our lunches). But she laughed at me and dismissed my request as being expensive, wasteful, and stupid.

Being newcomers to the United States, we didn't share the same sense of importance or style of celebrating national holidays and traditions as American families did. I remember experiencing a particularly embarrassing Thanksgiving as a young teenager. We were well aware of what Thanksgiving was and its tradition of having a number of foods available to feast on (which was likely to include turkey, stuffing, cranberry sauce, pie, etc.). But on this particular Thanksgiving, we had blackened, burned hamburger patties and boiled potatoes (my mother had a propensity for burning many fried foods when she cooked). I was OK with this because I knew that this is what we could afford, and so this was what we were going to have; it was not a problem with me. But as we sat at the kitchen table to begin our meal, the doorbell rang.

The unexpected visitors were a man from our church and his son (who was also one of my school classmates). They came as part of the monthly "Home Teaching" program that our church established (where two male church members are assigned to visit several other members' homes once a month to make sure everything is OK, find out if there are any problems or needs in these families, and to give a short spiritual message). My father invited them in, and they came into the kitchen to talk with us. I remember the shocked expression on the face of my classmate as he looked at the burned hamburger patty and boiled potato on the plate in front of me. This was *our* special Thanksgiving dinner. I felt humiliated. I dreaded knowing that he was now going to tell his friends and our other classmates about this, which would then become another source of laughter at my expense.

I also felt excluded from my brothers at playtime. My oldest brother was five years older than I was, and it seemed to me like he was almost always gone from our home. He would constantly be out among his friends in the neighborhood, playing, roaming, or doing whatever he did nearly the entire day. He seemed to come home only for his meals and then he was out again, experiencing his own life.

My second brother—the "middle" one, as I called him— was two years older than me. I soon recognized that this brother was well positioned in the family, and I was jealous of him. Besides having his own age-mates to play with, he was old enough to occasionally play and go exploring the neighborhood with our oldest brother and his friends. And—when they tired of him and sent him home (as boys are wont to do occasionally with younger hangers-on)—this middle brother was not too old to play with me and *my* age-mates. This usually wouldn't have been a problem, except that this brother very often liked to get my playmates to either run off with him and not allow me to follow, or to take my friends away in some game that included hiding from me so I wouldn't be part of their activities. Thus, he seemed to have the best of all three worlds—our older brother's friends, his own friends, and my friends—always having someone available to play with. During those few times that this middle brother *would* actually play with me one-on-one, I knew I was his "backup plan"—I "would do" if no one else was available. If something or someone else more interesting *did* come along, however, he was off in a flash, leaving me behind.

These early experiences and issues combined to develop a strong sense in me that I was different—I was definitely not the same as others around me. I didn't belong anywhere, and I felt that I was alone in the world.

I didn't realize until much later in my life that many children felt as I did, and that there are many lonely people in every crowd. But, as a child (and viewing the world through a child's eyes), the sense of isolation was devastating. My personal feelings of loneliness had a long-lasting effect on me (and on my behaviors) for many years.

Watching my baby boy in that hospital crib, I knew that I would do whatever I could to make sure that Erik knew that he would *never* be alone—that he was part of my life—forever. He would *always* be able to count on me to support him and be with him whenever he needed me. Even if he had no one else, *I* would be there.

At least, that was my promise.

Three

My Later Childhood I

*A torn jacket is soon mended; but hard
words bruise the heart of a child.*
—Henry Wadsworth Longfellow

O ver the years following our arrival in the United States, my mother had two miscarriages. After that, my first sister was born (when I was eight years old), and a second sister arrived sixteen months later. Our family was complete.

This sounds harsh, but sometimes I really did not know why my parents ever had children. When we were young, I got the very strong impression that we children were *not* wanted, we were in the way, and we were somehow responsible for many of our parents' problems in life.

Many years later—after I had become an adult and was able to somewhat separate myself emotionally from my childhood—I developed an imaginary scenario to help describe my early relationship with our parents:

I am very excited as I go to school for the first time. Here I am, five years old and starting kindergarten! I stand next to my mother as the school secretary asks questions while completing the registration form.

"Birth date?"

My mother tells her my birth date. I knew the month and day but not the year. I needed to learn that.

"Address?"

My mother gives it. I know that too. After all, we live just across the street from the school.

"His name?"

"Gunnar," she says, and then she spells it for the secretary.

"What?" I ask. This is a surprise. "My name is…Gunnar?" I'm incredulous. I remember hearing that word a few times in the past, but I had never associated it with my name—the representation of who I was.

"Yes," my mother says, brusquely. "Now be quiet!" My mother then turns her attention back to the secretary.

"But Mamma," I interrupt. "I thought my name was 'hold kjeft' (Norwegian for 'shut up')!"

"Hold kjeft!" she barks. She is now angry. I do as she says.

It isn't until after we return home when—following further questioning—I eventually learn that my oldest brother's name isn't 'Gå vekk!' ('Go away'), and my middle brother's name isn't really 'Ikke gjør det!' ('Don't do that').

That is a very informative and remarkable day in my life.

Of course, this imagined scenario didn't really happen, but it does describe the feelings that I had at that time. We were constantly yelled at and barked at by our parents. We seemed to always be in their way, and we appeared to be irritants to them.

But there were other events and behaviors that really *did* occur during our childhoods that affected us, and these included the verbal abuse—the name-calling—that we received. From the earliest times that I can remember up until we were at least in our late teens, we were often sworn at, yelled at, and called names. I recall well three specific names or phrases that our parents constantly utilized when we were very young (the following are the English-language equivalents of the original Norwegian words that they used):

"Shit children!"

"Devil children!"

"Assholes!"

These appellations would be thrown at us at the slightest provocation, and sometimes with no provocation at all. Both of our parents engaged in this name-calling, but I remember this abuse coming mostly from our mother. If a room was messy, it was because we were "shit children." If our parents couldn't find their car keys, it was the "devil children's" fault. If one of us had actually done something wrong, or even if our parents were merely having a bad day, it was because we children were "assholes."

I also noted that—even when I was a very young child— my mother seemed to especially enjoy the ability to use these words, to call us these vile names, when we were out in public. She seemed to like the power to be able to openly berate us, to chastise us, and to call us names in front of other people, all done while speaking in Norwegian. That way, she could say what she wanted and be as mean as she liked without others understanding her. We knew what she was saying, and that was what seemed to be important to her. By her tone of voice and her body language, however, I'm sure that those around us probably had a good idea of what was going on as well, but that didn't seem to deter her. For the most part, this method worked.

After we became adults, my middle brother pointed out something to me that I had not realized until he mentioned it. We had learned and knew many swear words in Norwegian, but he explained that we had never learned certain *other* types of words or phrases: kinder words, polite words. For example, while we were growing up, we had *never* heard or learned the Norwegian equivalents of:

"Please."

"Excuse me."

"Pardon me."

"I'm sorry."

"Forgive me."

After I thought about it, I realized that my brother was right. Throughout all of my childhood, I *never* recall hearing any of these words—expressions of thoughtfulness or consideration—uttered by our parents (either in English or Norwegian). These words and phrases were not part of our lexicon. Civility was not part of our childhood experience.

When we were young, I do remember that there were times when our mother showed us a kind side when she said that she loved us. This mostly occurred when we were crying after being hurt or injured during play or in other activities. Our mother would try to comfort us and get us to stop crying by showing empathy and telling us that she loved us. However, I don't think I believed her very much, since the name-calling and anger episodes were much more prevalent and intense.

This environment of an uncaring, unaffectionate atmosphere applied to everyone in our house, not to just the children. I never recall our parents referring to each other as *Dear* or *Honey* or any other endearing term. Instances of open hostility between our parents were rare, however, at least for the first several years that we children were present. A more apt description of their relationship at that time could best be described as a sort of "cold war" between them.

Although this antagonistic relationship constantly simmered beneath the surface, our mother sometimes did not take any great effort to hide her negative feelings for our father. My mother had a beautiful, strong singing voice, and she would often sing while doing housework or other activities at home. The songs she sang would mostly be traditional Norwegian songs that she had learned as a child, or they would be church hymns. But I remember a few times—when my father was not at home—that our mother sang "Release Me" over and over again. This song contained the following opening and closing verses:

Please release me, let me go,
For I don't love you anymore.
To waste our lives would be a sin,
Release me and let me love again.
...
To live a lie would bring us pain,
Release me and let me love again.

I did not think that my mother was singing this song merely because she liked the melody; I believe that this was an expression of her feelings toward her husband. I knew that my parents did not express or demonstrate affection toward each other when other people were present, but it was somewhat disquieting to hear my mother overtly express her sentiments in this way. In private, I'm sure that there was at least some sort of positive emotional connection between our parents; after all, they did have several pregnancies and children together during an earlier part of this period.

Besides the general name-calling and verbal negativity that all of us children received, I seem to have been subjected to some "special attention" from my parents. I don't know how my behaviors were so different than my siblings' actions or why I was otherwise singled out, but the following phrases appeared to be reserved just for *me* throughout my childhood and teenage years:

"What's the matter with you?"

"Are you crazy?"

"What's wrong with you?"

"Why can't you be normal?"

And my father seemed to particularly enjoy asking me, "Do we have to lock you up in a mental hospital or something?"

These cruel words not only reinforced the strong impression that I had developed about being significantly different—not at all like others—but they also taught me that I was mentally unstable, crazy, and/or insane. This led me to question almost everything I felt, said, or did, both within my family and with others. I constantly asked myself, *Are the emotions I'm feeling normal, or are they an indication that I'm mentally unstable? Did I say the right thing—like a normal person would—or did I talk like a crazy person? Were my actions socially acceptable, or was I doing something that an insane person would do?* These doubts and questions doggedly followed me throughout my early life.

The net effect of all of this was that I grew up feeling demeaned, worthless, and unwanted. I was socially inept, not having been taught how to be polite or to show consideration for others. I didn't know what love was; I didn't know how to show love, or even how *to* love—I'd never seen it. What I *did* see and understand was that I was unwanted, and I therefore thought that I was worthless, that I was garbage. After all, isn't garbage the rubbish in your house that you want to get rid of and throw away?

In my child's mind, that was what I had come to believe: I was unwanted, worthless, crazy garbage that should be—that *needed* to be—gotten rid of, thrown out.

In regards to the point raised at the beginning of this chapter, I'm sure my parents had children because they wanted to build a family. They likely did the best they could with the skills they had. But I also believe that—due to their temperament, their relationship with each other, and the hardships of life's circumstances—my parents were ill-equipped to raise children in a psychologically healthy environment.

Watching my baby in that hospital, I remember thinking: *My beautiful baby Erik;* you're *wanted,* you're *loved, and you're the most precious thing in the world to me. Someday, you'll grow up to be a great man, and you'll do magnificent things in the world. But for now, you're my precious little baby.*

I was determined to make sure that Erik's childhood was going to be *so* much different—and better—than mine.

Four

My Later Childhood II

*A child's life is like a piece of paper on which
every passerby leaves a mark.*
—Chinese Proverb

Although the verbal and emotional cruelty seemed to be the most prevalent and consistent factors in our home, our childhood also included a degree of physical violence. As far as my parents were concerned, I remember only a few times when I had personally been beaten or hit, but what I did receive was certainly more than enough.

One such instance occurred when I was around eleven or twelve years old. My father was very angry about something (I don't remember now what the fight was about), and he was hitting me while standing in the doorway to my and my middle brother's bedroom (which we shared). My brother was at his desk in the bedroom, and he decided to get involved (*that* surprised me).

"Why don't you just leave him alone!" my brother shouted as he entered the fray, swinging. Our father was very strong, and he threw us around like we were rag dolls. We were soon flying across the room and bouncing off the walls.

Apart from the beating we were receiving, something else happened during that incident that left a strong impression on me. During this fight, I distinctly remember my mother, standing behind our father in the hallway, actually *laughing*. Looking back on it, I'm sure that it must have been a nervous laugh (and probably not that she thought this situation was comedic), but what struck me at the time was that she laughed at all. I didn't really know what I expected from her; I thought perhaps she might try to protect us or intervene in some way to stop what was going on, but she didn't. Instead, she just said, "Boys, you can't hit your father!" and continued laughing.

Although my father had been physically aggressive with me on only a very few occasions, I remember that he had several more physical confrontations with my middle brother. There were ongoing hostilities between them that lasted many years.

My mother was no stranger to inflicting physical violence on us herself. One such instance for me occurred when I must have been about twelve or thirteen years old. It was a Sunday evening, and I had gone to church three separate times that day (we were Mormons): a one-hour priesthood meeting in the morning, another hour-long Sunday school class at noon, and a one-and-half-hour sacrament meeting in the late afternoon. That same evening, there was also a special fireside meeting being held at the local bishop's house that I was supposed to attend. After having already gone back and forth three times that day to the church for various meetings, I decided that I didn't want to also go to this fireside. My mother, however, told me I *was* going, and I retorted that I *wasn't*. This back-and-forth argument went on a few times, until my mother lost her patience with me and proceeded to beat the crap out of me, repeatedly slapping me and literally tearing the shirt off my back (because I had refused to change back into my Sunday clothes again). I was then forced to get dressed and was unceremoniously driven over and dropped off at the bishop's house by my father. I remember sitting at the fireside meeting that evening among about a dozen other young teenagers; I was trying to hide the red swelling of my cheek and hoping that the bleeding scratches on my back (where my mother had torn my other shirt off me) were not showing through my white shirt.

I don't remember anything about the lesson we were taught at that fireside meeting, but I well remember the lesson my mother taught me.

Church was a huge trigger issue with my mother. Back in Norway, she had attended the Lutheran Church as a child (with her family), and she later joined a Pentecostal church in her late teens. My mother converted to the Church of Jesus Christ of Latter-day Saints (also called LDS, or Mormonism) one year before I was born, and from that moment on she pursued that church and religion with a vengeance. In fact, it was her conversion to the Mormon Church that led her to emigrate from Norway and move us all to the United States. At that point in time, the LDS Church authorities advised my mother that she should move to "Zion" so that she could be closer to the base of their religion. She was also told that her children would have a better chance of eternal salvation if they were raised in that environment rather than to remain in Norway.

The Mormon Church has different definitions for "Zion." According to LDS scripture, Zion is the name of a future city that is destined to be built in Missouri in the "last days."

However, the Mormon Church hierarchy and membership have also often referred to Salt Lake City, Utah (which Brigham Young colonized in the mid-1800s with thousands of early followers) as Zion. So, in order to "go to Zion," my mother was told that she would need to move to Utah. She agreed.

After her baptism into the LDS Church, my mother engaged in a number of manipulative tactics to convince my father that they all needed to leave Norway—the country of their birth and the country for which my father had fought during World War II—and to immigrate to this new, foreign country.

My father was initially opposed to this drastic move; he saw no reason to leave his homeland. However, he later joined the Mormon Church himself, and the LDS leaders then pressured *him* to emigrate as well. Under this coercion from two fronts, my father finally relented. In just over one year after my mother joined the Mormon Church, we were all onboard a transatlantic passenger ship headed for America. Upon our arrival in New York City, we proceeded directly to Salt Lake City by train and settled there.

Another instance of violence directed at me from my mother occurred when I was in my midteens. It was during breakfast on a school day, and again, it began with an argument between my mother and me about something long ago forgotten. My mother became so angry that she picked up a butter knife and flung it across the kitchen at me. The blade hit me just below my right eye. I then stormed out of the house and began the over mile-long trek to school. Minutes later, when the stinging under my eye hadn't abated, I discovered that the knife had cut the skin, and it was bleeding. It wasn't too bad, however, and the bleeding soon stopped. I didn't tell anyone what had happened, but during school that day, several class-mates assumed I had been in a fight. I acknowledged that I had fought with someone that morning, but I didn't say who it had been with.

I don't know to what extent my older brothers had been recipients of our mother's violence (if any), but I do recall that my younger sisters were not spared. After graduating from high school, I recognized the need to get away from the toxic environment that was my home; therefore, I started attend-ing Utah State University in Logan, Utah (about ninety miles away). I lived in a dormitory on campus, occasionally returning home on weekends.

On one Friday afternoon, I arrived at our house to find both of my younger sisters crying in the backyard (they were about eight and nine years old at that time). Through their sobs, my sisters told me that they had done something wrong or had displeased our mother somehow, and she had sent them out to the backyard to find switches and branches from the trees and bushes there. They were instructed to obtain appropriate sticks, remove the leaves from them, and then bring them back into the house so that our mother could use these switches to whip and beat them. They also told me that this was not the first time they had had to do this.

I was horrified. I didn't know what to do. If I went into the house and confronted our mother, the consequences for my sisters and me might be worse. If I tried calling the police, that would have also meant doom for my sisters, and I was not sure the police would do anything about it anyway. Feeling sick to my stomach, I turned, got into my car, and drove back to the university, leaving my sisters to their fate. To this day, I feel regret and guilt over this; I should have done something—*anything*—to protect my little sisters, but I failed.

I now speculate that part of the reason for these behaviors on our parents' part—the swearing, the cruel and demeaning language, and physically violent treatment—may have stemmed at least partly from the stresses they were experiencing due to living in a strange, new country and trying to learn and adapt to a new culture and language. Maybe there were other factors involved in their lives that we did not know about or understand; I knew that we were poor, and so financial stressors also may have been involved. After looking back on this, however, I believe that we would still have been subjected to much of this behavior by our parents regardless of where we lived (whether it was in the United States or Norway) or what religion we belonged to. These behaviors they exhibited seemed to be the only ways they knew how to interact with each other, and with us.

In that hospital corridor, I made many promises to my little boy. I promised that *he* would be treated with kindness and love, and I promised that I would *never* be cruel or abusive to him. I also promised that I would protect him. He was *very* special, and I was going to make sure I treated him that way.

I knew that I had a lot of personal psychological and emotional baggage to overcome, but I wanted to do everything I could to make sure that Erik would have a *much* better life than I had.

Five

Baby Erik

Children will not remember you for the
material things you provided,
but for the feeling that you cherished them.
—*Richard L. Evans*

A fter his birth, Erik and his mother remained in the hospital for five days. Each time I came to visit, I watched my son intently, always amazed at this new life—this seemingly perfect little baby.

When it was time to go home, I remember Janet getting into the obligatory wheelchair and the nurse placing our little son in her arms and then handing me a plastic bag full of take-homes from the hospital. I also remember pausing at that moment, half expecting someone to now give us the instruction book on how to care for and raise this beautiful little child. After all, don't all major appliances, cars, and even toasters come with written "care and use" instructions? And this was a *baby*—much more valuable than any of these other items. Unfortunately, no instruction book was forthcoming.

We did not have the usual grandmother (or any other relative) at our house who could help out for those first few weeks; it was just the two of us. But that was OK; we were going to figure it all out (even without a book). My self-instructions were simple: keep my baby boy clean, keep him fed, keep him warm and safe, and most especially, *love* him. If I could do those things well, I thought everything else would fall into place.

After taking my new family home, I went to the store to buy some baby formula. Janet had decided not to nurse Erik because, as she put it, it was "gross" to have a baby sucking on her nipples (nor did she want to use a breast pump). I knew that breast milk was healthier for babies, but I didn't say anything about Janet's decision. I secretly welcomed the opportunity to be involved in the feeding process myself, because this would give me the chance to hug and hold Erik close to me as he ate, and I cherished that physical contact.

The first night in our home, I was somewhat reluctant to put Erik to bed (we lived in a single-wide trailer house, and his room was down the hall from our bedroom). I wondered, *Will we be able to hear him when he wakes up? Will his cries be loud enough to wake us?* We had never had a baby in our home before, so these were unknowns. That evening, after he went to sleep, I gently placed him in his crib. We then went to bed ourselves.

The next morning, I awoke in a mild panic—Janet and I had both slept straight through the night! Had Erik cried? If he did, had we missed it? Had he gone hungry? Was he all right? I hurried into Erik's room and found him lying in his crib, still sleeping contentedly. My heart settled down. Our baby had apparently slept through the entire night, and I thought, *This isn't so bad!* However, our luck did not hold out, because after that first night Erik seemed to place himself on his own schedule, sleeping no more than two hours at a time (often less)—every day and every night—for many months. Eventually, his sleeping periods lengthened so that he did not wake as often, but there was not to be another uninterrupted full night's sleep for either of us for almost that entire first year.

As Erik grew, I watched him closely. In light of his difficult birth and the temporary lack of oxygen, I wanted to see if there were any developmental delays. I noted when he was able to focus his vision on an object and to follow the object with his eyes. I saw when he was able to react to a sound and turn his head to find its source. He learned to reach out to touch objects and then grab them. I watched him as he was able to push himself up off the bed and to roll himself over, front to back and then back to front. As the months passed, I noted when he was able to sit up, stand by himself, and then start walking. In virtually all aspects, Erik appeared to progress either on target (as compared with others his age) or even a little ahead of schedule. I was satisfied that there appeared to be no discernable brain damage or problems as a result of his birth process. My precious little Erik seemed to be a normal, healthy boy.

Over the following months, Erik grew and his personality blossomed. He and I enjoyed many hours and many days together. I loved it.

It was when Erik was about six weeks old that I was first able to make him laugh. I tickled his stomach until his muscles tightened up, and then he started laughing. One of the best sounds I've ever heard was my baby's first laugh. After that, I did many things that would bring laughter and joy to my little boy. Sometimes, Erik would not like his food, so I'd make a game with his bottle or the spoon of food until he laughed (occasionally, these games and his laughter would interfere with, and extend, the time it took for him to eat).

Occasionally, Erik would have a sore bottom when I was changing him, and so that turned into a game as well. I would talk to him in a strange voice or make faces at him, and his laughter would distract him from his discomfort. After the changing, I'd hide at the end of the crib and play peek-a-boo with him, which he always thought was a riot. Erik had a beautiful laugh.

Erik had a few health issues that necessitated doctor visits. The first medical visit (other than well-baby checkups) was due to excessive crying for hours and hours, for no apparent reason. This was causing enormous stress and lack of sleep for all three of us. Colic was the diagnosis, and medication was prescribed. It seemed to work, because every time we gave it to him, Erik soon became lethargic and groggy, and then fell asleep. After a few episodes of this, I read the label on the medicine bottle, and noticed it contained a certain percentage of alcohol (I don't recall how much). We were actually drugging him!

During his infancy, Erik had a couple of bouts of congestion and high fever. These episodes really worried me. Twice, his temperature went up to the 104° F range, and I was at a loss of how to bring the temperature down (we still had no instruction book!). Once, a call to the hospital and a conversation with a nurse helped, as she gave me advice on bringing down fevers. After that, I found I didn't need to go into a panic each time his temperature rose. One thing that amazed me, though, was that Erik seemed to be able to handle a high fever quite well. When he did have a high temperature, Erik was still generally the same child he was before, the only difference being that he seemed a bit more sluggish in his actions and reactions. On the other hand, whenever *I* had an elevated temperature (such as 103 or so), *I* was completely devastated; I would be in bed with chills and sometimes I would ramble in incoherent speech. In short, I could not function.

During one of his visits with our family doctor, we were told that we should take Erik to a pediatrician because he seemed to have a depressed sternum and there might not be enough room for his chest organs to grow and develop. A few days later, the pediatrician who examined him told us that his chest was fine, but he said that we should have his heart murmur evaluated. That soon brought a trip to a hospital and more tests with all sorts of wires and machines. The eventual diagnosis was that it was an "innocent" heart murmur. We were told that it really was not a matter of concern and he should eventually grow out of it. Relief! Making sure that our babies are healthy (and remain that way), can be a very nerve-wracking task.

As Erik became older and was able to crawl (and was given the run of the house), he embarked on his own adventures of discovery and amusement. I remember one such instance when I was watching television in the living room. Erik was in the adjoining kitchen, and I was not paying a lot of attention to him at first. At one point, I heard a soft blowing sound from him, followed by giggling. These sounds were coming from the kitchen. Then, a moment later, another soft blowing sound and more giggling. This piqued my curiosity, and I went to see what was happening. I found Erik lying down on his stomach on the kitchen floor, watching a spider crawling away from him. Erik softly blew at the spider, which then retracted its legs and formed a ball as it was scooted along a few inches on the smooth linoleum floor by his breath. Erik laughed at this. The spider would then slowly unfurl its legs and start to frantically try to get away as Erik scooted himself closer and blew again. I started to feel sorry for that poor spider.

When Erik was about seven months old, Janet and I scheduled a two-week winter trip to Norway (over the Christmas and New Year's holiday). My wife had never been outside of the United States before, and I wanted to show her where my family came from and to possibly let her understand a bit more about me and my family's past. We found a very good price for airline tickets, and I made the reservations. We decided not to take Erik with us because we thought it would be too difficult—both on him and on us—to take a baby on such a long and tiring trip. Erik was to stay with his grandparents (Janet's parents) while we were gone. However, almost as soon as the plane left the ground, I started to miss Erik so very much. After we landed at our destination, I quickly approached a ticket counter and moved up our scheduled return fights a few days so that I could come back to Erik again sooner.

I had brought along some photos of Erik on our trip so I could share and show off our beautiful child. I remember the surprised look on one relative's face when—after asking if they wanted to see some pictures of Erik—I pulled out a thick stack of probably sixty or seventy snapshots of my little boy to share with them. I was proud of my boy.

Ten days later, we returned and immediately went to pick up Erik (a three-hour drive from the airport). There were hugs and kisses all around, and regret on my part that we left him. I decided that it would have been worth the trouble to have taken him with us.

It was when Erik was quite small that I recognized the importance of having traditions. I wanted to institutionalize practices that we could look back upon with fond memories later in life, events that would help us to remember what we meant to each other and the love that we shared. One of the traditions I started with Erik was to take a photo of him on each of his birthdays at the same moment of his birth: 3:22 p.m. When he became older, I knew that these could (and would) probably be staged photographs, but, at least when he was young, we could see what he was doing at that particular minute, and I thought it would be interesting to record part of his history this way.

I also began another tradition of writing a personal letter to Erik on each of his birthdays—a letter describing what he was doing at those points in his life, such as his interests, his likes and dislikes, what activities he enjoyed, and so forth. But I especially wanted to use these letters to tell Erik how I felt about him—how much I *loved* him—at these different times. I planned on saving these letters and presenting them to Erik when he was older, perhaps when we was eighteen, or when he went to college, or maybe when he got married. I thought he would like to know what my thoughts and feelings for him were each year as he grew.

I dutifully took his one-year-old photo at 3:22 p.m. on his birthday. He was sleeping soundly, on his stomach in his crib. I also wrote his first letter. I told him what he liked to do, what his favorite toys and foods were, and what words he could say. I also wrote about how much he meant to me and how much I loved him.

Later, I carefully put this letter and the photo away, wondering how Erik would respond to them after he grew up. I hoped that he would like them.

Six

How Did I Get Here?

Another belief of mine; that everyone else my age is an adult,
whereas I am merely in disguise.
—*Margaret Atwood*

I had experienced what I perceived to be a miserable, emotionally destructive childhood. I had an extremely low self-image (I thought I was worthless), and I considered myself very deficient socially and emotionally. So, how did I get from that desolate, low point all the way to the position of being married and becoming the father of a beautiful, precious baby? I had never thought such a thing would have been achievable. How could that have possibly happened?

If there are such things as miracles, then this is probably one of them.

When I was growing up, I was actually *frightened* of girls. I had very little interaction with girls when I was in grade school and junior high school, and I didn't know how to relate to them. A great portion of this was likely due to my extreme shyness and insecurities, but I believe it was also partly due to my experience with the Mormon Church. From a very early age, children in this church are taught that there are very specific gender roles. The boys learn that they will be "priesthood holders," that they are destined to be leaders both in the home and in the church, and that they will have powers given to them by God to perform ordinances and blessings in God's name (and with God's special authority: God's priesthood). The girls learn that their basic goal and mission in life is to help provide a spiritual and loving home, both for her husband and for their children. The highest calling for girls is to become wives and mothers. This training becomes more formalized when, beginning at age twelve, boys and girls are put into segregated programs and meet separately during parts of their church services.

I thus learned that girls were very much different than boys, and since girls were so dissimilar and distinctive, I didn't really learn how to relate to them normally. I consequently viewed girls as being quite *special*, but not in a healthy way. In my mind, it was almost as if females were of another race altogether—perhaps even from another planet. This training, combined with my own shyness, meant that I was always tongue-tied around girls, not knowing what to say. And when I *did* say or do something, it usually came out wrong, and I constantly felt like I was making a fool of myself. I envied those guys who could talk and associate comfortably with girls; I certainly couldn't.

When I was in high school, there came a point when I was naturally becoming interested in girls and the prospect of dating. But how can I do this when I had such a low opinion of myself? The answer: *with extraordinary determination and effort!* And—I might add—I was usually not very successful at this endeavor.

It was an enormous and deliberate struggle for me to bridge the gap between reality and my perceptions at that point—to look upon girls as regular human beings who have the same aspirations, concerns, wants, and needs as everybody else. At that time, I did not understand the simple fact that we are all just *people*.

When I was sixteen years old (after observing a certain girl—Natalie— from afar for many months), I fought to overcome my fear and took an enormous leap of effort and faith: I actually asked her for a date. This was toward the end of my sophomore year in high school, and I was painfully aware that nearly all of my friends and acquaintances had already been dating—both as couples and in groups—for quite a while. I was the odd ball, and getting up the courage to enter this alien world was very difficult for me.

Natalie lived not far from my house, and we had known each other since we were both about eight years old (ever since my family moved into that neighborhood). We attended the same church, and we were in the same grade. I really liked this girl, and I enjoyed being around her. She always seemed to be in such a good mood, and she usually had a smile on her face. She had a bright, positive attitude, and I secretly wished that some of that would rub off on me.

We lived just over a mile from our high school, and we walked home in the same direction. Natalie often walked with a girlfriend who lived next door to her, but she occasionally went home alone. During those instances when she was by herself, I tried to arrange it so I could walk with her part of the way. If I saw Natalie walking ahead of me, I'd hurry to try to catch up with her. If she was behind me, I'd slow down and dawdle until she caught up to me (it never occurred to me to just ask if I could walk home with her). When we were walking near each other, I tried to engage in some small talk with her—when I dared to speak to her at all.

After several days of meeting like this, I finally built up my courage. My stomach was in my throat when I forced the words out and asked Natalie if she would like to go to an upcoming school dance with me.

I carefully watched Natalie when I put the question to her, and I noted her reaction. Her eyes blinked and her head jerked back a bit as if she had been physically hit in the face. I took that to mean that she was totally surprised by my question, and she had not previously viewed me as possible date material. I thought, *This isn't good,* and I immediately regretted my rash behavior. *Why am I so foolish as to think that anyone would want to go out with me?*

After a few moments, Natalie told me that she would have to ask her father's permission first, and she would then let me know. I viewed this response as a way to gently let me down so that she could politely refuse my request later. I mentally kicked myself for my presumptive impertinence.

Nevertheless, after a few days had passed, I was quite surprised—*astonished,* actually—when Natalie told me that she *would* go with me to the dance. This was certainly a milestone for me—my first date!

The evening of the dance arrived and the date went well, but I was incredibly nervous throughout the evening (besides my not really knowing how to dance). I did enjoy being with her, and I imagined what it would be like to actually have a girlfriend (if it ever got that far). Maybe I *could* be normal after all! Looking back, however, I now see that I likely came across to Natalie as being dreadfully emotionally fragile and very needy—because I *was.*

We went out together a couple of times after that, and one date I remember quite well was our last. We were at a drive-in movie and sitting close to each other on the front seat of my parents' car. I had my right arm around Natalie. Even though we had dated a few times, we had never kissed. I lightly rubbed her cheek with my left hand, and then I gently kissed her cheek. I remember thinking, *This would be a good time to turn your head so we can kiss,* but she did not. Natalie sat with her head rigidly facing forward, and she didn't move a muscle. I then backed off from my amorous efforts and didn't try kissing her again. I felt rejected and humiliated. Again, I thought how stupid I was to think that anyone would want to spend time with me, let alone like me enough to actually *kiss* me. My self-loathing sank its insidious roots even deeper into my psyche, where it flourished.

Several weeks later, I did ask Natalie for another date. This time, she declined. I don't recall her reason for refusing my invitation, but whatever it was, I viewed it as a rejection of *me*; she didn't want to be around me. With my extremely poor self-image, how could I blame her? I didn't want to be around me either! Even though I really liked her and enjoyed being with her, I never asked her out again; I didn't want to put her in the uncomfortable position again of having to refuse future invitations from me.

On reviewing this situation, I don't know why Natalie didn't kiss me, or why I read so much meaning into this one experience. At that time, we were both members of the Mormon Church, which vigorously discouraged its young, unmarried members from engaging in actions or activities that might lead to potential "chastity" problems. Kissing was viewed as one of these hazardous activities. I don't know if Natalie was following this advice by not kissing me, or if she was not really *into* me. Either way, however, I viewed it as reinforcement of the experiences and feelings I had learned well while growing up in my home: I was unlovable, I was unwanted, and my mere presence was often an annoyance to others.

During my high school years—and most of my college years—I dated very few times. I saw only two more girls when I was in high school (one of these was a blind date arranged by the girl's mother, who knew my mother), and one other girl when I was attending Utah State University (we had known each other from high school). All of these were only one- or two-time dates. On some occasions I did not call the girl again, and sometimes the girl declined a follow-up date invitation. I convinced myself that each of these girls realized that I was not someone worth getting to know any better. I couldn't blame them for not wanting to see me again.

When I was a senior in high school, however, I *did* have my first kiss—sort of. I had dated a sophomore girl a couple of times; her name was Brenda, and she also had that bubbly, outgoing personality that was very attractive. When I took Brenda home after our second date, I was hesitating at her front door, being *very* nervous. At that point, Brenda took the initiative and gave me a quick "pity" kiss (a peck, really) on the lips, and then she opened her front door and slipped inside. It was nothing romantic, but rather a way for her to end an awkward moment and send me on my way. I'm sure she just wanted to get rid of me and go inside her house. I got it.

By the time I graduated from high school, I realized that I was eighteen years old and not only had I never had a girlfriend but I hadn't even had a *real* kiss with a girl. I felt socially backward, and I continued to believe that *all* of the normal experiences of life were passing me by. That thought really troubled me, and I was becoming obsessed with it.

While attending classes and living on campus at Utah State University (USU), I was acutely aware that I was still very inexperienced in relationships with girls and women. The loneliness and isolation I had felt ever since I was a young child continued. People around me were growing into adults with *lots* of experiences—experiences that included *much* more than a single, small peck of a pity kiss. I believed that everyone else in the world was progressing with their lives, moving on, maturing, and developing relationships. Everyone but me.

At about this time, I actually became upset when I learned that Natalie—the first girl I had dated in high school—was getting married. That news distressed me, although it shouldn't have. I think I probably held some unfounded hope or dream that we might eventually get together again. I seemed to be harboring a secret wish that Natalie would be there, waiting for me when I graduated. Even though I had never maintained any direct contact with her over the last couple of years, I had thought that I needed to finish college and embark on a career first, before I could even think about marriage (and that was still years away). Perhaps, at that time, I imagined I would contact Natalie and we would start seeing each other again.

Regardless of my unstated fantasy, Natalie was progressing with her life, becoming a wife and probably a mother, building her own household and family. As for me, I remained emotionally stagnant, stuck in my childhood, trying to make occasional, fleeting efforts to attempt to connect with someone to help me pull out of the quicksand of depression in which I was mired. I desperately wanted to become an adult too.

It was during my third year at USU when I first noticed Janet. I don't remember what initially attracted me to her, or what made me think I had any chance with her. Janet did not have the same type of extroverted, bubbly personality that had previously attracted me to other girls; she seemed to be a quiet person. Janet lived in a nearby women's dormitory, and I saw her occasionally with one or two girlfriends. I noticed her on campus as well, and I never saw her with another guy. I later realized that this was an important factor for me at that time—that any person I might be interested in must *not* already be in another relationship. In my mind, I was a nobody, and I therefore could not even *think* about successfully competing with *anybody* in the world for a girl's affections. I would *always* be someone's last choice (if I was ever a choice at all).

When I eventually got up the courage to ask Janet out, she accepted. Again, I was surprised that someone did accept. After that first date, there was a second, and then a third. I thought that here—*finally*—was somebody who seemed to actually accept me. My attraction to her was likely the fact that she didn't turn me down when I kept asking her out. We continued to date, and we eventually kissed. In fact, this is the first person I had *really* kissed, romantically (and one might say that she actually taught me *how* to kiss). I realized that I was in an odd situation; I knew that most of the people around me were in deep relationships and were having sex, and here I was, just learning how to *kiss*. I knew I was still socially and emotionally far behind the rest of the world.

After a couple of months into this relationship, I went with Janet to visit her parents during Thanksgiving break. Their home was about four hundred miles away in western Colorado, so this trip involved a lot of driving and an overnight stay at a motel each way. It was at one of these motels that we eventually had sex. I won't go into details about this experience, other than to say it was...bizarre. But, as they say, things can sometimes improve with experience. Over the next few months, this relationship continued.

Although I no longer considered myself as an adherent of the Mormon Church, their influence on my actions, behavior, and belief systems was apparently still quite strong. Beginning when I was a child, there remained within me some remnants of the instruction and indoctrination I had received over the years. One of these is that premarital sex was a horrendous thing to do; it was just *wrong* on so many levels. The church even taught that the seriousness of committing the sin of sex without marriage was next in severity—in God's eyes—to the sin of committing *murder*. Even though sex was an activity that most people all over the world were doing—and I *wanted* to be like other people—my ingrained teachings told me that it was immoral. I felt guilty.

I reconciled this issue in my mind by deciding that having premarital sex was just that: *pre*marital. To me, this meant that sex was OK as long as we were *going* to be married, and my having sex with a girl meant that I was obligating myself to marrying her. I never did explain this line of reasoning to Janet, mainly because I knew that she would have laughed in my face. She was sexually experienced with many partners before I met her, and she certainly never viewed having sex with someone as a commitment to get married.

Besides experiencing a sense of obligation and guilt as reasons for wanting to marry Janet, I also harbored the belief that I had now somehow found and connected with the *only* person in the world who was even *willing* to have sex with me. In my mind, if I didn't marry Janet, I would *never* be married because there was no one else on Earth who would even consider being with me in that way.

I don't remember how I originally broached the subject of possible marriage with Janet, but after a while we eventually came to an understanding that we were to be married. I'm not certain of Janet's motivation, but I believe it may have arisen from a basic desire she had to not be alone in life herself. I really don't think real love played a role in either of our decisions.

The following weeks were quite difficult. At one point, Janet told me that she couldn't get married because she still had strong feelings for a friend with whom she had been sexually active (and who was bisexual). In fact, she had been fantasizing about him when we were having sex (I discovered this when she once called out *his* name when we were being intimate). That event initiated a sixty-mile car trip for both of us to go to see this friend in person. After a short visit, Janet told me that after seeing the two of us together, she no longer had romantic feelings for this former boyfriend, and things were back on track with me. I actually won one!

Events such as these continued, however. Janet would occasionally raise an objection to our marriage, and I would steadfastly argue *for* it, trying to use reason and logic. I think she realized on some level that we were not a good match, but I was desperate (after all, I believed no one else would have me). Eventually, Janet would cave in. However, in the evening before we were supposed to get married (which was on my twenty-first birthday), she resolutely called the whole thing off. That initiated hours of further reasoning (and even pleading) on my part, but to no avail. Janet didn't yield.

Early the next morning, I went over to Janet's dormitory apartment and made one last pitch. I think I had finally worn her down because Janet then changed her mind again. Later that day, we went to the town's local justice of the peace (along with a couple of Janet's roommates as witnesses), and we were married. Neither one of us had told our respective families of our plans beforehand.

At that point, I believed I had accomplished what I needed to do. I had followed my personal moral code, and I had married the person I was having sex with. I didn't feel guilty anymore.

However, I was also acutely aware that I entered into this marriage with a fatalistic attitude: I actually did not expect it to last very long. I knew that there were major problems and issues between us that would not likely permit a permanent or even a long-term relationship. I remember thinking that we would be together at least six months, but I certainly did not think that our marriage would last more than two years. Even within this limited projected time frame, I went ahead with the marriage. I believed that Janet was the only person in the world who would even consider marrying me, and I didn't want to lose this one and only chance to find out what married life was like, even if it lasted only a short period of time. Of course, Janet knew nothing of these thoughts or suspicions.

Our marriage—or rather, the time we lived together—lasted longer than the two-year maximum lifespan that I had originally given it. We still had our problems, of course, which were only amplified as time passed, and these problems negatively affected our relationship. It was within this atmosphere (approximately four years into our marriage) that Erik was conceived. It was a surprise.

Janet had always stated that she had never wanted to have children. She had previously given two reasons for this: First, she said that she did not, and never did, have any *desire* to be a mother; and second, she could not tolerate experiencing physical pain (especially that of childbirth).

When she found out that she was pregnant, Janet immediately opted to have an abortion, and she asked her doctor to make an appointment with another physician who would perform the procedure. Even though having a child had not been a driving force for me in my life—it was not a major life goal or dream for me at that moment—I liked children, and I enjoyed being with them. Over the years, I became quite fond of the idea of becoming a father and taking care of and raising a child. I told Janet that I would like to have this child, but I added that the decision was ultimately up to her (it was *her* body, after all).

About a week later, Janet surprised me when she told me that she had decided to go ahead with the pregnancy. She never did explain why she changed her mind, but I was delighted. The appointment for the abortion was cancelled.

This became an unexpected opportunity for me to experience an entirely new aspect of life, one that I had previously thought was unattainable for me: to have a child and become a father, to actually have my own family, to try to be *normal* and have a normal life. I was finally going to be a real adult.

It was from this inauspicious beginning that my precious little Erik came into my life.

Seven

The Marriage Ends

*The pain experienced during a breakup is as individual
as the trillions of people who go through it.*

—*Tigress Luv*

When Erik was about twenty months old, the relationship between Janet and me deteriorated drastically. The feelings between us were not what they should have been, and in fact the atmosphere in our home was destructive and harmful—to each other and to Erik. Partly because of my own selfishness (I very much wanted an emotionally healthier life than I had experienced up to that point, and I convinced myself that I was somehow entitled to such a life), I initiated divorce proceedings. I did not want to live like my parents did.

Once it appeared that a divorce was inevitable, Janet initially recognized that Erik would be—as she put it—better off with me than with her, and she agreed that I would have primary custody of our son and that she would maintain visitation rights. I was very happy about this. However, after a conversation with her sister, Janet changed her mind and demanded sole custody for herself. There were no reasons given for this change of heart, but I suspected it was done to punish me; it was payback for my wanting to split up. This was a tragic turn of events for me, because those were the days when judges automatically granted custody of small children to the mother in divorce cases without regard to the best interests of the child (unless there could be some obvious or gross misconduct demonstrated).

At that point, I had to make a decision. Did I want to stop this divorce process so I could keep Erik and have him with me? He was the only bright spot in my life, the one thing that had made me happy. But the negativity, the anger, and the bitterness between Janet and I was palpable, and definitely not healthy. Also, I had somehow convinced myself that I might have a real chance at happiness in other parts of my life—an opportunity to have a normal relationship with another person. Sometimes, it surprised me to think that I might actually have "deserved" happiness. I was soon torn apart, trying to weigh the pros and cons of my situation and my decision.

In the end, I continued with the divorce. In hindsight, this was probably a huge mistake, as it set into motion a series of unforeseen events that changed many people's lives.

As this divorce process continued over the following weeks, I came home from work one day to find both Janet and Erik gone. This occurred without warning on that particular day, but it was not really unexpected.

I was instantly alone again; that all too familiar feeling from my childhood returned. Even though this situation had occurred as a result of *my* choices, it still hurt—a lot.

I tried to assuage the pain of my loneliness by dating a coworker who I started seeing shortly after my breakup with Janet. This relationship became serious rather quickly, but by the time the school year ended, this woman had returned to her ex-husband (from whom she had recently divorced). That was certainly not the right time in my life to start seeing someone else, but I couldn't tolerate the pain of the loneliness that I was experiencing.

Soon after Janet and Erik had left, I found out that they had gone to her parents' house in Colorado. It took approximately eight hours to drive the over five hundred miles that now separated us. This put a huge impediment in my ability to visit my son; instead of seeing him every other weekend (as is usual in divorce cases), I could only hope to see Erik briefly on long weekends or during extended vacations.

Although Janet had insisted on having primary custody of Erik (and took him with her when she left our house), she did not actually have him living with her. A few weeks after moving away, Janet enrolled in a master's degree program at a university in Provo, Utah, about halfway between her parents' home in western Colorado and my home in southern Idaho. While Janet was staying, she had decided to leave Erik with her parents rather than letting him be with me. That action reinforced my opinion that she was using her custody of our son to punish me.

Between the time that we split up (in February) until his birthday in May, Erik and I had the opportunity to visit only twice. When I first saw him again (after having been away from each other for about six weeks), Erik didn't recognize me. That was very painful, but he slowly warmed up to me, and within an hour we were well-acquainted again. The second time I picked him up for a visit (about a month later), it seemed like it took a few minutes before Erik recognized me and came to me. My third trip to see Erik was on his second birthday. He was excited to see me as soon as I walked in the door. He immediately recognized me and jumped up into my arms! This time,

I was taking him home with me; we were going to be together for the entire summer.

On our trip back to my house in Idaho that afternoon, I stopped the car when it was about twenty minutes after three o'clock. I got Erik out of the car and we stretched our legs. At precisely twenty-two minutes after three, I took the second picture to put in his "what I was doing on my birthday" album. That night, I wrote my second letter to him. I was excited about maintaining these traditions.

That was the beginning of what I thought was going to be a wonderful summer; my son and I were united again. I was going to be happy for at least these several weeks that we were going to be together.

Eight

The Summer to Remember

In the depth of winter,
I finally learned that within me there lay an invincible summer.
—*Albert Camus*

I got a new job in Salt Lake City and moved down from Idaho to Utah at the beginning of that summer. I did this so I would be closer to Erik when I had to drive to get him again for my weekend and summer visitations. Although the official visitation rules were that I would have Erik with me for six weeks each summer, Janet agreed to let him be with me for the entire summer. I was ecstatic.

Likely because of being taken back and forth between me and his grandparents' home during the previous months, Erik developed a fear of abandonment. He gave the strong impression that he was afraid that we (or I) might leave him and *not* come back. Whenever I *had* to leave him with somebody (such as with a babysitter), he would scream and cry and fight as I walked away, and it broke my heart to leave him that way. When I did return, the babysitter always told me that he soon calmed down and was fine after I left. Nevertheless, the separation process was still painful for both of us.

A couple of times that summer, I took Erik to a nursery at a Presbyterian church that I was thinking of joining (so I could attend the one-hour service in the chapel). He let me—and everybody else—know that he did *not* want to be left there. The second time I left him at the nursery, I knelt down and told him, "It's OK; I'll be back. Be good."

At that point, Erik put both of his little hands on the sides of my face, and he turned my head so that we directly faced each other. With tears streaming down his face, Erik looked straight into my eyes and softly sobbed, "Go, go, Pappa. Go." He wanted to go with me, he didn't want me to leave him there, he wanted us to stay together. That was the last time I attended that church—I couldn't leave him at their nursery any more during services. The emotional cost to me of leaving him for that hour was too much for me to bear, and I didn't want to keep upsetting Erik.

That summer, I tried to give Erik all the love I could. I was only trying to be fair, because Erik had so much love and kindness in him that I knew I couldn't return everything he gave. Up to that point, I had never seen a little child who was as fond of hugs and kisses as Erik was. He *loved* to give hugs, and he *loved* to give kisses.

I was living in an apartment that summer, and I didn't have Erik's baby crib there. At that point, however, he was two years old, and he deserved his own bed. Until I had time to get him one (it would have to be a child's bed that was special to him) I let him sleep in my queen-sized bed with me. When we went to bed, I would tell him to go to sleep, and he would dutifully put his head down and cover up. Various times during the night, he would occasionally reach out and touch me, probably to reassure himself that I was still there. Once, I was lying on the bed, facing him. I felt his hand reach out in the darkness and touch my face. He felt around a little bit, found my nose, and then he *pinched* it—hard! "Erik!" I said. He just laughed.

Soon after going to bed at night, Erik would sometimes sit up in bed and look over at me.

"Hug?" he'd ask.

I'd turn over and—as Erik put his little arms around my neck—I'd give him a big, squeezing hug. He'd smile and lay back down. A few minutes later, he would prop himself up on his elbow, look over at me and ask, "Kiss?"

I'd turn over and give Erik a kiss. Sometimes, I'd give him a big, wet kiss all over his face (which would make him laugh), and then a nice, little kiss on his cheek or forehead. After that, he'd lay back down with a smile on his face. A little later, he'd say, "Hug?" or "Kiss?" again, and the process would repeat. This could go on for quite a while; it depended a lot on whether or not he was tired and ready for sleep. These activities would sometimes keep me awake much longer than I wanted, but how could I scold him for showing love and wanting love in return? Besides, *I* needed and cherished *his* love.

That summer started off being a good one. School was out, so it was just him and me, together every day.

We prepared meals together; I asked him for various utensils, and he got them for me, and sometimes he would help in stirring or mixing ingredients.

We set the table together; I gave him dishes and silverware and told him if it was "for Pappa" or "for Erik." As he took the item, he'd make a small nod and repeat, "Pappa" or "Eh-Eh" (he wasn't able to completely articulate his name at that time), and put the item at the correct spot on the table.

We watched television together; Erik's favorite program was *The Muppet Show.* Erik sat on our rocking chair in front of the television set and watched the program, mesmerized by the colorful characters and their antics. A couple of times, Erik became upset at the episode's conclusion and would begin to cry because he wanted it to continue. However, he soon accepted the fact that the show lasted only a half hour, and there would be another show the following week.

We went places together. Erik especially enjoyed going to the zoo. On our first trip there, Erik was particularly impressed with the elephants. During the time he stayed with his grandparents in rural Colorado, he had lived on a cattle ranch with them. He had seen many cows, steers, and bulls there. And when Erik saw an elephant for the first time, he was quite impressed; he turned to me, pointed to the elephant, and said, "*Big* bull!"

There were occasions when I was short-tempered with Erik—times when I made him cry (besides those instances when I had left him with babysitters). Of course, these were not on purpose; I *never* wanted to hurt my little boy.

When Erik was a little baby (and was eating strained baby food), there came one day when he didn't eat—for the entire day. After I came home from work one day, Janet told me that he refused food that morning as well as throughout the day. She then went to work for the evening (she was on swing shift). I tried to get Erik to eat, but he refused me as well. When it got closer to his bedtime, I decided that he had to eat *something* (I couldn't just let him *starve*), so I sat him in his high chair, got a jar of one of his favorite foods, and started to feed him. But whenever I put a spoon of food in his mouth, he spit it out. I then put the food back in his mouth, and he spit it out again. This went on for a while until Erik started crying. I kept on trying to feed him, which only made him cry even more. After a while, I felt so bad that I couldn't continue. I later decided that Erik was not in any danger of starving, and that he would have started eating on his own when he felt ready to do so. Where was that instruction manual for the proper care and treatment of babies that I needed so badly?

Another occasion I remember occurred when we were living in the apartment complex that special summer. The apartments there were arranged so that the doors for four apartments opened onto the same landing. Of the three other apartments connected to my landing, two subscribed to a local daily newspaper, and the delivery person would just drop them on our common landing, not in front of the intended recipients' doors. Once, when I came home with Erik, he was so excited to see these newspapers that he quickly picked one up and proceeded to walk into our apartment with it.

"No!" I scolded. "Put it back!"

As soon as those words came out of my mouth, I felt remorse. Erik was only trying to be helpful, and he didn't understand my anger. He began to cry at my sharp words, and my heart broke. I knew what I did wasn't right. I held him and apologized. After that—whenever we saw that a newspaper was near our apartment door—I whispered to Erik that the paper wasn't ours, but he could be a helpful "big boy" if he would put it in front of the neighbor's door for me. He did so without a problem. I hated myself for not handling the situation that way the first time.

Generally, the summer was going very well. I was living part of my dream—my purpose in life. I had my son with me, and although other aspects of my life were torn apart and in shambles, at least *we* were together.

I was totally unprepared for what was about to happen.

Nine

The Accident

A moment in time can change many lives forever.
—Author

It was a beautiful July evening that summer. It was a Thursday. I had taken Erik with me (along with my youngest sister) to see the original *Star Wars* movie. As we were enjoying the air-conditioned theater, Erik sat contentedly on my lap with our box of popcorn on his own lap.

He was at first enchanted by all of the sounds and sights and excitement of the movie, but as the evening progressed, Erik became quite tired. He first laid his head back on my chest while continuing to watch the film. He later turned around, laid his cheek on my shoulder, and went to sleep as I held him.

After the movie ended, I carefully stood up and walked out of the theater with Erik still asleep. One teenage patron observed this and remarked, "Wow! He slept through *that?*" Toddlers can sometimes be very sound sleepers.

When we got to my car, I carefully placed Erik in the middle of the front seat and buckled him in, unintentionally waking him in the process. My sister got in on the passenger side. On our way back to my apartment, we first stopped at the drive-up window of a fast-food restaurant to pick up some hamburgers for my sister and me, along with a hot dog for Erik (one of his favorite foods). As soon as we got the sack of food, Erik took it from me and placed it on his lap. I suppose he decided that he was in charge and was going to take care of the food until we got home. That was OK with me.

I drove down one of the main streets of Salt Lake City. There were three traffic lanes in each direction and a speed limit of thirty-five miles per hour.

As I approached the intersection at which I needed to turn, Erik suddenly leaned over onto the bag of food that was on his lap. Seeing that he may be crushing our food, I tried to get Erik to sit back up, but he refused. He didn't say anything; he just continued to lie on the sack. I just let him be.

Our car became the first car in the intersection's left turn lane. All the traffic lights in our direction were red. When the cross-street traffic eventually stopped, the turn lane control light gave me a green arrow, and I proceeded forward. Just as our car was almost through the intersection, I briefly noted a pair of headlights approaching on my right—*very* quickly. These headlights belonged to a car that was driving outside of the three lanes of cars that were stopped at the intersection. It was a fraction of a second between the time I first saw the oncoming headlights and when I felt the impact of our cars colliding.

At that moment, everything went black.

I woke up as a policeman was reaching over me, trying to remove Erik from the car.

"I can't get him out!" he shouted. "He's stuck!"

I was surprised at this statement. I reached down beside me and pushed the release button on Erik's seatbelt, and the policeman then pulled him from the car.

But my other surprise—and deep concern—was that Erik was *unconscious*. I didn't know what was in the car that he could have hit his head on.

I looked over to my sister and saw that she was awake. The other vehicle had hit us on the right-front corner of our car—closest to her—but she said she was OK.

I got out of my car and followed the policeman who had taken Erik. There were already several police cars surrounding us, so I wondered how long I had been unconscious.

First, the officer laid Erik on the trunk lid of one of the police cars; it looked like he was trying to examine my son. He then placed Erik on the backseat of the patrol car while I watched them through the car's rear window. My anxiety increased, and my mind raced. *What's wrong with him? Why is he unconscious? How badly is he hurt?* As I watched, I noticed that my hand was cut and blood was dripping from it onto the car's rear window.

I stepped away from the patrol car for a moment and quickly scanned the area. The right-front corner of my car was completely smashed, and the entire front half of my car was actually bent to the left. My car was also pointing in the wrong direction. This indicated that the collision must have occurred with enormous force. I soon found the other car. From its position, it looked like it had actually bounced back several feet from the impact point with my car. The entire front end of the second car was smashed and there was a hole in the front windshield on the passenger's side, as if someone's head had gone through it.

I saw what appeared to be a young man lying on the street in front of that car, with somebody in civilian clothes holding a bloody cloth to his forehead. I assumed this injured person was the driver of the other car, and I immediately thought about what I could do to injure him further, right there in the street. I remember thinking, *What the hell did you think you were doing? How dare you hurt my little boy!* I found out that this individual was not the driver but the passenger (whose head had partially gone through the windshield). I learned later that the car's driver had left the accident scene "at a pretty fast pace" (according to one officer) and had to be retrieved by the police.

Soon ambulances and paramedics arrived. When they placed Erik in one of the ambulances, I climbed in as well. The attendant didn't want me to be there and shouted for a policeman to remove me. I clearly told him, "He's my son, and I'm going with him." The paramedic accepted this, and we drove off.

On the way to the hospital, I looked at my little Erik, lying unconscious on a very big stretcher. I noticed that one of his front teeth was missing, and the hole it left was bleeding a little. *Not a problem,* I thought. *That's just one of his baby teeth. His adult tooth will grow in just fine.* Erik coughed once, and some vomit came out of his mouth. Other than that, he didn't move.

When we arrived at the hospital, they placed Erik on a gurney and wheeled him into an examining room. I began to follow him, but the staff directed me into an adjoining room. I protested and said I wanted to stay with Erik.

"Don't worry. He'll be all right," a nurse said as she gently pushed me toward the other room.

I was placed on an examination table and they started to inspect my wounds. Besides my concussion, all I had was a severed tendon in my left hand. I lay there, worried about Erik. After a few minutes, I did the only thing I could think of to try to help: I began rattling off Erik's medical history, speaking out to no one in particular. When I mentioned his depressed sternum, a nurse took notice and left to pass this information to those who were attending to Erik in the other room.

The hospital staff then asked if there were people they could call for me. I gave them Janet's phone number as well as the numbers for my middle brother and our parents.

A couple of hours later, I was told that Erik was being transferred to another facility in the city that specialized in pediatrics: Primary Children's Hospital. They said that Primary would give Erik more specialized care there than was available at this hospital.

Eventually, I was admitted to the hospital for surgery on my hand as well as for observation for my concussion. I was told that Erik had arrived at Primary and had been placed in their intensive care unit. He was in a coma. They said that he was receiving excellent care there, and he shared a nurse with only one other patient in that unit. I was informed that I could call anytime to speak with his current duty nurse, which I did several times over the following days. The nurse on duty would listen to me as I talked about Erik, but whenever I asked specific questions about his condition and prognosis, she deferred and said that I should talk to the attending physician about those things. I knew that was not a good sign, but I still held out hope for a full recovery.

During this time (when Erik and I were at different hospitals) my father woke up with a certainty that Erik would recover completely from his injuries. All that was needed, my father thought, was to *immediately* give Erik a priesthood blessing.

The Mormon Church teaches that its members who hold priesthood authority (which includes virtually every male member who is age twelve or older), have the ability to give healing blessings to those who are sick or injured, through the power and authority of Jesus Christ and God. The church teaches that these blessings can—and often do—cure the person who receives the blessing. Stories of success in these endeavors are touted during the monthly Fast-and-Testimony meetings that are held in every Mormon congregation. This is what he wanted to do.

My father later told me that he was suddenly woken from a deep sleep with the definite impression that—if he would *immediately* go to Primary Children's Hospital and give Erik such a blessing—then his grandson would be completely and instantly healed. The LDS Church had repeatedly taught him (over the nearly thirty years he had been a member) that such promptings are from the Holy Ghost, and that they should be heeded.

Since church members are instruced that such blessings should be done in pairs, my father telephoned (and woke up) his Home Teaching companion and asked for his assistance in this endeavor (who then agreed). These two men thus proceeded to visit Erik in the hospital in the middle of the night.

My father had faith that the inspiration to perform this ordinance came directly from God, through the Holy Ghost. In fact, his faith was so great that he had even taken a small blanket with him so that he could wrap Erik in it and bring him home after the blessing.

At the hospital, the Home Teaching partner anointed Erik with previously consecrated virgin olive oil. Both men then placed their hands on Erik's little head and my father gave the blessing, commanding that Erik be cured and healthy.

Of course, nothing happened; Erik's condition was unchanged and he remained in a coma. Eventually, my father and his companion left the hospital empty-handed.

When my father went to that hospital to give Erik a blessing, he had *faith*—a *lot* of faith. I would say that the amount of his faith far exceeded "a grain of mustard seed" (Matthew 17:20). And he wasn't attempting to move any mountains; he was just trying to make his grandson well, but it didn't work.

After this incident, my father (who was an ordained High Priest at that time) lost trust in the LDS Church's claims that their priesthood powers were from God and that they gave its members the ability to cure the sick and injured.

After three days, I was released from my hospital. My middle brother picked me up, and I asked him to drive me directly to Erik's hospital.

It was so sad when I saw Erik. My precious little boy lay in the large hospital bed, unmoving. He had numerous tubes and wires connected to him. Equipment was beeping and machines were pumping air in and out of him. I stroked Erik's soft cheek with my hand, tears running down my face.

"Pappa's here," I told him. "Pappa loves you."

My little boy only lay still.

After some minutes, a doctor appeared and briefly explained Erik's condition: Erik had received a significant blow to the head, which caused his brain to swell. The skull was not broken, however. The doctor said that it would have been *better* if the skull bones had been broken in the accident, because that would have given the brain room to expand without damaging itself. I immediately wondered why they hadn't opened his skull surgically to relieve this pressure, and then reset the bones once the swelling had subsided, but I didn't say anything—whatever damage there was had already been done. The doctor did say that they had given Erik medications to try to reduce the swelling, but they had been ineffective.

The doctor continued by telling me that because of the swelling within the unbroken skull, Erik's brain had been under so much pressure that it was severely damaged. He said that an EEG had been performed that morning, which indicated that there were no brain waves present.

I was stunned.

"Isn't that what they call brain death?" I asked plaintively.

The doctor only nodded.

"We'll do another EEG tomorrow, and if there are no brain waves present then, we'll disconnect his life support system," he said. But then he added, "We really don't expect any change."

I stayed with Erik for a long time, and I came back later that evening. I talked to my little boy about many things. I told him how much I loved him and how much he meant to me. I told him how glad I was that I got to know him.

I also smoothed down his beautiful hair and caressed him. I kissed him, and—through all those wires and tubes— I touched, held, and rubbed those parts of him that I could reach: his stomach, his hands and feet, and his arms and legs.

I felt so sad for my helpless little boy on that bed—my precious little son. Without hesitation, I would've *gladly* exchanged places with Erik. In return for Erik's life, I would've *happily* forfeited my own. *Absolutely.* If there really was such a thing as magic in the world (and if I could access it), Erik would still be alive.

When I arrived at the hospital the following day, the doctor informed me that—as expected—there were no brain waves from that morning's EEG. He said that they were going to disconnect Erik's ventilator soon. I was asked to wait in a private room nearby when this happened.

After about ten minutes, a nurse brought Erik to me, wrapped in a soft, blue blanket. She carefully placed my little son in my arms and left. My two sisters were with me at that time, and we all cried. One sister took him from me and held him for a minute or two, and then gave him back. They both then left, leaving the two of us alone.

Although Janet had come and visited Erik several times during his stay at this hospital, she had decided not to be present during this transition.

I sat alone in that small room, knowing that I was holding my beautiful son in my arms for the last time. He looked different now. I saw what death looked like: his skin was gray and his lips were dark.

I hugged Erik and sat him on my lap. I tried to play a game with him—the same game we'd played hundreds of times before. In this game, I hold him on my lap and count, "One, two, three, and…whoops!" as I move my knees apart when I say the last word. Erik then drops a few inches between my knees as I catch him. He always laughs and enjoys this silly little game. Only this time when we played, Erik didn't laugh or giggle. I guess I was secretly hoping that Erik would suddenly come to life with laughter, but he didn't. Erik's lifeless body didn't respond.

The situation finally became clear to me: My little boy will *never* laugh again, and he will *never* giggle or be happy. We can *never* play together again. That one moment in time—that instant when the two cars collided—changed the whole world for Erik and for me.

After only two years and two months of life, my beautiful, precious little boy was gone.

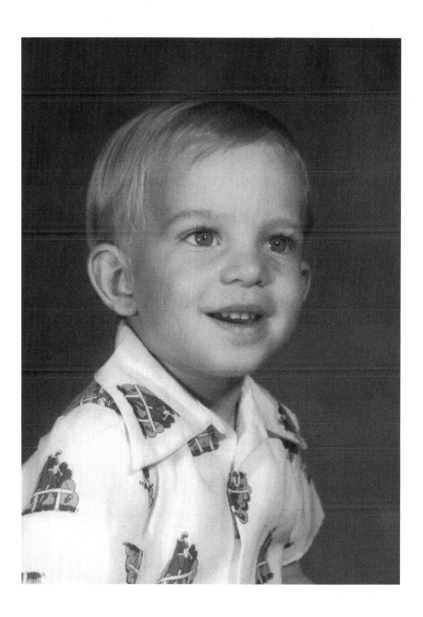

Ten

Coping

You can't avoid pain, but you can choose to overcome it.
—*Unknown*

The difficulties of trying to cope with Erik's death and its aftermath began the moment he died.

It was extremely hard to realize that Erik was really gone, or to even acknowledge that all this was actually true, that it was real. What if this was just all a terrible nightmare? Maybe this was one horribly sick joke? How *could* it be true? The center of my life—my reason for living—was gone. How do I even live with this? What do I do?

My struggles of coping with this situation began with the hospital staff telling me that I needed to arrange for a funeral home to take care of Erik's body. Since his death was the result of a criminal act, I was also told that the mortuary would first need to take Erik to the medical examiner's office for an autopsy. Once that was completed, the mortuary would retrieve him and prepare him for a funeral (if that was what we wanted).

How do I do all that? I was only twenty-eight years old. What did I know about mortuaries and funerals? I had only attended one funeral in my life (the father of my friend, Gary), and now I was supposed to make all these arrangements? I remember asking these questions aloud in the hospital's intensive care visitor's waiting area (after a nurse had retrieved Erik's body from my arms), and a woman sitting across the room uttered a painful groan when she overheard me. She was obviously a parent of a child on that floor, and I remember feeling regret that my comments upset her, but these issues were overwhelming me. This was another major turning point in my life when I desperately needed an instruction book. What do I do in this situation? I had absolutely no idea.

In retrospect, it was ironic that I—who had spent most of my life being *so* concerned with missing out on the experiences of life (dating, kissing, getting married, having children, being a father, etc.)—was now experiencing those parts of life that *no* one my age should be experiencing: the death of his child. This was one part of life experience I *didn't* want and I didn't need. I certainly would've given *anything* to forego *this* experience.

Not knowing what else to do, I blindly chose a funeral home from the telephone book Yellow Pages and called them from that hospital waiting room. The person who answered the phone likely sensed my anxiety and trepidation, and the necessary information was received with compassion. Neither they nor I foresaw the new problems that were approaching.

Of course, this was an entirely new world for me; I didn't know about all the things that had to be done for a funeral and burial. How could I? Over the next few days, my family helped me as I made contact with a cemetery, a headstone company, and a florist. I even had to decide what clothes Erik should wear. What *do* people wear when they are buried? I had no idea. I decided to buy a new outfit of the same clothes Erik was wearing when we had the accident (his old clothes were bloodied and had been cut away from him in the hospital emergency room). The shirt had an image of Ernie—one of the characters from his favorite television show.

While discussing funeral arrangements with Janet, she suddenly informed me that she wanted Erik cremated with no inurnment in a cemetery. This surprised me. No, this *shocked* me. Of course, we had never previously discussed any possible funeral arrangements if Erik should die—that was an unimaginable event. But, now that the unthinkable *had* happened, Janet was adamant that he be cremated rather than have a burial. She said that the divorce granted her primary custodial rights to him when he was alive, and that she should therefore be the one to decide the disposition of his body, now that he had died.

I *couldn't* agree to that. I had already purchased a burial plot for him. I wanted to have a place where I could visit his grave, a place of focus where I felt I could talk to him, and a place where I could feel somewhat close to him. When I bought Erik's grave, I also purchased the grave next to him. This was for me. If I couldn't be with Erik anymore in this life, at least we could be together in death.

I expect I was also still influenced by the religious teachings of the Mormon Church regarding the Resurrection, and how the souls of those who have died will one day be reunited with their bodies and they will then "rise up from their graves." In a way, I suppose I wanted both Erik and I to "rise up" at the same time, so that we would be together again.

This disagreement between Janet and I continued unabated, with both of us adamant and unyielding. At one point during this dispute, I thought of a possible solution: I would put a notice in Erik's published newspaper obituary indicating that he would be cremated. This would signal to Janet that I agreed to the cremation, but—in actuality—I would then surreptitiously have his body buried in the chosen cemetery.

The obituary was published as planned, but my attempted deception didn't work.

I received a call from an exasperated mortician (who had found himself caught in the middle of this argument) requesting a joint meeting with myself and Janet in order to rectify this situation. Janet arrived with her parents, and I with some members of my family. At this meeting, the funeral director indicated that we needed to resolve this issue quickly, and he added that whichever side "wins" in this dispute would be held solely responsible for the financial costs of the mortuary and funeral services involved. Janet and her parents immediately backed down. I was relieved; Erik was not going to be cremated, and his body was going to a cemetery.

There were many people at Erik's funeral service, including colleagues and friends from my previous job in Idaho. There were also members of my immediate and extended family who lived in the area. But neither Janet nor any members of her family came.

I wanted to speak at Erik's funeral service and to share my feelings for him, but I was advised that I was probably not going to be able to talk—and make any sense—in the emotional state I was in. Instead, in keeping of my tradition of writing those periodic letters to Erik, I wrote a final letter to him. An Episcopalian priest, who had been on the staff of the hospital to which I had been admitted after the accident (and who attempted to comfort me that first evening), officiated at the funeral, and he read my letter to Erik. Afterward, at my request, the priest put the letter in an envelope and placed it in Erik's coffin with him.

My last letter to Erik read:

Dear Erik:

When you were born, I had been waiting five years for you. And when you finally arrived, I felt that my life was complete; I had a purpose.

It was hard for me to wait for you to be released from the hospital after you were born. I wanted to watch you grow and develop.

After you were with us, I suffered with you with your colic and your colds. When we found out about your heart murmur, we took you as fast as we could to specialists. I watched your development progress from the day you were born to the day you first smiled and first laughed, when you first learned to stand up, sit, and crawl. And we all took great pride and joy when you took your first step. And my heart almost broke with pride when you first called me Pappa.

After you learned to run, there was no stopping you. You would run when it was time to change you, and you'd giggle all the way while we were chasing you. You even took to climbing the bookcases, falling off a time or two.

I tried to prepare everything for you. I wanted to ensure that you had four basic things to prepare you for your adult world: heritage, good health, intelligence, and enough financial resources to let you start any career you chose. For your heritage, you received your middle name—Kristian—which was the name of my grandfather. It was to help you get interested in your cultural heritage, your background, in learning why you have the genes you received. For your health, I made sure you had the finest medical care available. For your intelligence, I tried to help you grow properly, developmentally. And for your future finances, your bank account was started within a week of your birth.

So you were wanted, prepared for, and were in the process of being the best person I could make of you.

In return, you gave me more happiness in two years than I thought was possible.

So, Erik. Even though it's been decided that I can't have you anymore, I want you to know that you'll not be forgotten. You had a special quality in that you gave love to everyone you touched, and they will all remember that.

I'll remember your "loves," your big hugs, and those wonderful kisses you learned to give, especially at bedtime.

I'll remember you, every action, everything you ever did or said. I'll remember you. There can never be another you.

I would like these words to be remembered by all who ever knew you:

Never was one loved more, or more full of love, than Erik.

Good-bye, my son,
Pappa

It may have been presumptuous on my part, but I had the last line of this letter engraved on his headstone: *Never was one loved more, or more full of love.* It described exactly how I felt.

It was a surreal experience at the cemetery. There I was, saying good-bye and burying the most important person in my life. No, it was more than that. I was burying the most important person in the *world*. To me, Erik was the most precious, beautiful, wonderful soul that ever existed, and now he was gone. I knew that humanity was significantly lessened by Erik's death, and yet…it seemed like nothing changed, nobody outside our small circle there seemed to notice the import of this event. Everything was going on around us as if nothing happened—the sun was still shining, birds were singing, the wind was blowing. Cars were still driving on the busy street nearby, honking at each other. The world just kept going on like nothing happened.

Standing there at the cemetery, I remembered the lyrics of Skeeter Davis's 1962 song, "The End of the World" (RCA Records). The words from this song include the following:

Why does the sun go on shining?
Why does the sea rush to shore?
…
Why do the birds go on singing?
Why do the stars glow above?
Don't they know it's the end of the world?
It ended when I lost your love.
I wake up in the morning and I wonder why everything is the same as it was.
I can't understand, no I can't understand why life goes on the way it does.

Although parts of this song specifically refer to the loss of a romantic love, I identified very strongly with most of the lyrics. I couldn't understand why there weren't major changes in the world—in fact, there didn't seem to be *any* changes—when the most precious person in it had just died.

After returning from the cemetery, I soon noticed something very wrong at my parents' house. Janet had apparently been in the house while we were all at the funeral (she knew where my parents hid their extra key outside), and she had removed *every* picture of Erik that she could find. If there were snapshots of only Erik, they were gone. If there were photographs of Erik with others in the picture, the part with Erik on it was torn away. This was a major attack on my psyche at a time when it was already so fragile, and I couldn't understand this behavior. I thought this assault was possibly just another way that Janet chose to try to hurt me—and it worked.

I talked with Janet about this incident a few months later. She said that she did this to try to remove any trace of Erik's existence. She told me, "The only way I can deal with this is to pretend that he never existed—to forget that he was ever born."

I know that people react to and deal with grief in different ways, and if this is what Janet had to do to personally cope with this unimaginable loss, then so be it. I thought she could have removed all traces of Erik from her *own* life—if that's what she needed to do—but I didn't think she should have done this with others' memories. I did have some pictures and memorabilia of Erik remaining at my apartment, but I certainly missed all those that had been left at my parents' home.

In my own case, it would have been impossible to forget that he ever lived. I wanted Erik's life to mean *something*; I wanted his life to *matter*. It mattered very much to *me*, and I wanted it to matter to others as well.

It was *extremely* difficult coming back to my own apartment after Erik died. As I walked through the rooms, I saw many reminders of my little boy, each one tearing away at my heart. There was the rocking chair he sat in while we watched television. There was his chair and his place at the dining room table where we sat and ate our meals. He would no longer help me set the table or clear it afterward. There were his clothes on the closet shelf and in the dresser drawers. I could still smell him on these clothes. His toys were scattered in different places all over the apartment. After we put away these toys each night, Erik always dutifully spread them out to many different places during the following day. Now, these toys would never be scattered again, nor would they ever be used at all. I saw the bed where we slept, and I knew that he would never again ask for hugs and kisses at night; I would never again feel his little arms around my neck.

I cried.

I did find one very special trace of Erik remaining in the apartment. On the sliding glass door that opened from the living room to the patio, a perfect, full handprint remained. It showed how small Erik was, and how beautiful his little hand was. During the following three years I remained in that apartment, I never cleaned his handprint off that glass door. It was my reminder of the life of my little boy, my precious son who lived with me for part of that wonderful—and dreadful—summer.

Eleven

Grief

Man Was Made to Mourn
—*Robert Burns*

My personal grieving process began on that city street the moment I regained consciousness after the accident. I was *very* scared when I saw Erik unconscious. I saw that there was a possibility that he had been seriously hurt, and that frightened me. This fear grew as time went on and Erik didn't regain consciousness and his condition didn't improve. When they moved him to Primary Children's Hospital for better treatment—and he didn't recover—a feeling of dread came over me. This fear only increased over the following days until my worst, unthinkable terrors were confirmed, and they disconnected little Erik from his life-support system.

During the following few days (when I had to try to cope with arranging a funeral; arguing with Janet; interacting and dealing with police, lawyers, and insurance companies; talking with family members and well-wishers, etc.), I essentially functioned in a haze that was overlaid by many emotions, all of which seemed to occur in a jumble and made me feel as if I was literally going insane. Many new feelings and experiences flooded me during that time.

After the funeral and burial, I noticed that my emotions seemed to coalesce into several distinct feelings: sadness, depression, despair, confusion, anger, and numbness. I found that there were times when a combination of at least three of these emotions (sadness, depression, and despair) would overwhelm me. Regardless of where I was, these feelings would gradually build up to an intolerable level, and I would sometimes begin to cry during part of these episodes (regardless of where I was or what I was doing at the time). Eventually, these feelings would fade, only to be replaced by a growing, intense anger. Following these periods of powerful emotions (sadness/despair, followed by anger), I would eventually become emotionally exhausted. At that point, I wouldn't feel depressed or angry, nor would I be happy or sad—I just felt *numb*. It was likely only during these unemotional periods that I appeared to be "normal" to others and able to function somewhat effectively in my daily life. Then, after another interval of time, the feelings of sadness and depression would begin creeping back into me and the endless cycle would repeat.

Following Erik's death and its immediate aftermath, I rotated through these brutal emotional periods of despair-anger-numbness multiple times each day. As time went on, however, the frequency of these emotional cycles lengthened, so that it would take weeks (and eventually months) to complete one entire sequence of this sadness-anger-numbness cycle. I also found that the intensity of these emotions generally lessened over time (although I would still experience spikes of severe anger or depression, and occasional tears).

There were moments, however, when I experienced a brief respite from this emotional roller coaster. Sometimes, just at the moment when I woke up in the mornings, there was a fleeting second or two when I actually felt somewhat *normal*. At those moments, I thought that I had no problems and everything was right in the world. This delightful feeling soon changed as the dark curtain of sadness descended and enveloped me for the remainder of the day.

After Erik's death, I found that I had difficulty getting to sleep at nights. I often lay awake for hours with my racing thoughts chasing each other in circles in my mind. I learned to cope with this by deliberately waking up early each morning, being as busy as I could during the day, and then I'd make an effort to stay awake very late into the evenings until I was so exhausted that I would quickly go to sleep when I went to bed at night. The next day, I would repeat this sequence. Consequently, I often ended up feeling quite fatigued during my waking hours because I wasn't getting nearly enough sleep at night (but at least I could get *some* sleep that way).

Another emotion that I experienced (and still feel, to some degree), is guilt. I remember specifically one instance—about a week after Erik's death—when I was up late, watching *The Tonight Show* with Johnny Carson. During his monologue, Johnny told a particularly funny joke, and I laughed out loud. I surprised myself with that laugh, and I immediately felt guilty about it, thinking, *What right do I have to laugh? My son is dead, and he* can't *laugh anymore!* With time, however, I learned that I *can* laugh—it's OK.

Even though I had allowed myself to laugh again, I was aware that it was different. Whatever happiness I now felt was muted when compared to what I experienced before Erik's death. It was as if a dark blanket had been placed over my emotions, covering them and restraining them from their full expression. My moments of happiness never reached the levels they had previously occupied. It was as if an undercurrent of sadness permanently infiltrated my soul.

I do experience a level of guilt that remains with me always; I feel guilty that *I* didn't die in that accident, and I feel very guilty that I didn't protect Erik from harm (since that was my job as a father). I continue to live with those feelings.

Of course, I felt overwhelming loneliness immediately after Erik's death; I missed him terribly. I believe this profound sense of loneliness and loss led to two dreams I had during that period. In one dream, Erik came to me, and I remember being completely overwhelmed with pure *happiness* and joy—my son was back! We played together with his toys and we played with each other; we ran and chased each other, and we rolled around on the floor together. It felt like this lasted the entire night. Unfortunately, I knew that this was only a dream when I was experiencing it, and I knew it would end when I woke up, but I thoroughly enjoyed it while it lasted. When I woke up that morning, I was surprised that I was *exhausted*—I actually felt physically *tired* from the activities during my dreams that night. The positive afterglow from that evening lasted several days and calmed me emotionally for a time.

A couple of weeks later, I had a second dream about Erik. In this one, I dreamt that Erik was a young adult—he appeared to be about twenty years old or so. It was a very brief encounter this time, as he came only to give me a message. He said that he was sad that he died so young, and he wished that he could have lived longer. He added that he was all right and that I shouldn't worry about him. He also said that he loved me. After that, he was gone. This second dream may have been still another remnant of my early Mormon Church programming, as they had taught that, in the "Spirit world," we are all adults, regardless of the age we are when we die.

In all the years since Erik's death, I have never had any other dreams about him. This has been extremely disappointing and sad to me, as there have been times that I've been *desperate* to see him, to feel him, and to talk to him again—to just spend a few moments with him, even if it only occurred in a dream—but it has never happened again.

I have sometimes tried to accurately describe the feelings that I experience as part of my grief, my mourning. Throughout many years of professional training and education, I have attended various universities and earned advanced degrees. In that process, I have read literally thousands of books covering a wide range of topics, including psychology. I have read *millions* of words. Despite all of this, I frankly cannot find any words in the English language that would adequately describe the depth and breadth of the painful emotions a parent feels when one has lost a child due to death. It is literally indescribable.

A few times over the years, I have met with different counselors to help me try to cope with issues and challenges in my life. Counselors are trained to try to identify and put a name to their clients' emotions and to reflect these feelings back to them in an effort to build a sense of empathy, understanding, and trust within the therapeutic setting. On one occasion—as the client in a counseling session—I described some of the experiences I'd had (and the emotions I had felt) that were associated with the death of my child.

After I had finished, the counselor began with, "I'm not going to even *pretend* that I have any idea of what you're going through."

That was an honest assessment from this counselor, and he was right. Unless people have experienced these horrible events themselves, they have *no* idea what is going on in our minds, our hearts, and our souls. Just as when I was a child, I felt very alone; no one seemed to know or understand what was happening to me.

After Erik died, a few people offered to lend me their ear in case I needed to talk. I believed that these were sincere offers, and I certainly *did* need to talk. I needed to talk about Erik, and tell people what a beautiful and precious child he was. I needed to talk about how much I loved him and how much I missed him. I also needed to talk about my emotions and feelings, and what was going through my mind; I needed to know whether or not I was going insane.

I did ask to speak with two different acquaintances on separate occasions within a few weeks after Erik died. During both instances, the friend was sympathetic and tried to be helpful. After several minutes into these discussions, however, I noticed that their responses stopped and their eyes widened slowly as they listened to what I had to say. It was clear that they had no way to relate to what I was saying; they didn't know *how* to help. I quickly realized that I needed more than what these well-meaning friends were able to provide.

I had a childhood friend—someone I'd known since we were eight years old—named Gary. Gary and I had been classmates since the third grade. Gary had married a woman named Suzann a few years after I had gotten married, and his wife came into their relationship with a small boy, Seth, who was born before they met. A couple of years into their marriage—when Seth was just seven years old—he was hit by a car when riding his bicycle near their home. He died from his injuries.

After I saw that these other well-meaning people couldn't really help me, I contacted Suzann and asked if I could speak with her, since she had also lost a child to death. Our single visit lasted about an hour, and it was time well spent. We both knew what the other one had experienced—and was still experiencing. We understood each other. I was in pain, and now I knew I wasn't alone in my feelings. I knew I wasn't going insane.

Since I saw that Suzann was still alive and still functioning after experiencing her own hell on Earth, I thought that there was a chance that I might eventually be able to do the same.

At that point, I recognized that there may actually be hope for me in surviving this.

Twelve

Anger

The world needs anger. The world often continues to allow evil because it isn't angry enough.

—*Bede Jarrett*

Anger is often described as a negative emotion, one that eats away at (and is very destructive to) the person holding it or experiencing it. However, anger can also focus one's efforts to make positive changes, either individually or within society in general. It can be said that anger—generated by perceived injustices—was a strong motivator that brought about the positive changes during the civil rights and women's rights movements in the past. It can be used to right wrongs.

As part of my personal grief, I felt a *lot* of anger. This emotion is recognized as one of the factors involved in the grief process described by Elizabeth Kübler-Ross (the well-known psychiatrist who specialized in the subject of grief and dying). However, I was not angry at a god or at fate for what had happened. My anger became quite specific; I was angry at the person who caused the accident that killed my son. I later became angry at the societal circumstances that allowed this tragedy to continue to happen.

Soon after the accident, I was told that the other driver was drunk, with a blood alcohol content (BAC) level that was above the legal limit at that time (which was then set at 0.10). Even though that driver had left the scene of the accident—apparently with a broken leg—he was quickly found and sent to a different hospital than Erik and me. When the investigating officer gave me the personal information form of this other driver (which is normally exchanged when traffic accidents occur), I found out that his name was Jimmy S. and that he was twenty-three years old. The officer mentioned that Jimmy had a history of arrests for alcohol and drug-related issues. Also, I soon discovered that the car he was driving was not registered, his driver's license was not valid, and he had no insurance.

This was an easy target for my anger.

Several people told me at that time that my anger was misplaced. They said that this was an accident and that I should not dwell on it, put it behind me, and move on. I was told that nothing I do will ever bring Erik back. Others said that the offending driver's conscience would somehow punish him, and that, "He will have to live with this the rest of his life." Some suggested that I needed to "forgive" the other driver.

I found it quite odd that these comments came from people who didn't know anything about Jimmy and his record, and they apparently didn't know me either. I *couldn't* let it go. I had to see that "justice" was done, and to me justice meant that a person who causes the death of another person should be punished.

A few weeks after the accident, Jimmy was finally arrested and charged with manslaughter (a second-degree felony) for causing the death of Erik. Upon conviction for such a charge, the penalty included incarceration for a period of between one and fifteen years. Bail was set at $15,000 (a substantial amount at that time). I was told that the charges and the high bail were due to the egregious factors involved. I thought that this high bail would assure that Jimmy would remain incarcerated for a while—perhaps even weeks—before he could bail out of jail. A couple of days later, however, Jimmy's public defender was able to get the bail reduced to $3,000, and a $300 payment to a bail bondsman set him free.

In the meantime, I did some research and soon discovered that there were approximately forty to forty-five thousand traffic deaths *each year* in the United States. That surprised me. I also found out that approximately *half* of these traffic deaths involved high levels of alcohol consumption. That *really* disturbed me. I was amazed that such devastation should be allowed to continue.

I met with the assistant prosecuting attorney who was assigned to handle Erik's case, and I found her at a small, cluttered desk in a very large room that contained many other desks, attorneys, and other staff—none of whom apparently rated the amenity of a cubicle. During our short conversation, this attorney's cat walked back and forth across the desk and over the files scattered there. Although this setting did not engender a lot of confidence, I still hoped that she would be effective in prosecuting the case.

At this meeting, I learned that Jimmy's charges had been reduced; he was now charged with automobile homicide, a third-degree felony (which, by the way, is on the same par as a charge of resisting arrest), with a potential penalty of zero to five years in prison. I was told, however, that those who were convicted of automobile homicide were very rarely incarcerated; instead, they almost always received probation.

I was quite surprised at this information (and at this attitude of the court system). "So," I asked, "a person can get drunk and kill another person and essentially get away with it? Without going to jail?"

The prosecutor explained that this was different than having used a knife or a gun to kill someone. Since this involved a car, it was viewed as an accident by the judicial system, and the fact that he was drunk was another mitigating factor—he was *less* responsible for his actions because of his inebriated state. I saw no difference between getting drunk and driving a three-thousand-pound automobile up and down busy city streets at a very high rate of speed (without any regard for the safety of others) and getting intoxicated, taking a gun, and shooting blindly into a crowd. Both actions are equally lethal, and I thought both should be punished equally. But that was just me, I guess.

Surprised at the likely prospect that Jimmy was likely to receive only probation, I questioned the prosecutor further.

"Because of what happened that night," I began, "can Jimmy be charged—or at least *ticketed*—for reckless driving, speeding, driving outside the lanes of traffic, running a red light, leaving the scene of an injury accident, driving under the influence, driving without a valid license, driving without insurance, and operating an unregistered car on the public roads? He did *all* of those things; he had *all* those infractions."

The prosecutor told me that all of these charges were wrapped up in the automobile homicide charge. I was stunned. It seemed probable that Jimmy was not going to do *any* jail time (with the expected sentence of probation), and he wasn't going to be required to even pay for a speeding ticket for what he'd done. That didn't seem right to me. However, I did learn that upon conviction of automobile homicide, Jimmy would lose his driving privileges for one year. *Wow,* I thought. *That shows what value this society places on a human life!*

The trial was held several months later, and, for the first time, I was able to see the person who killed my son. Jimmy was haughty and arrogant before and after each day's trial session and during the breaks. His manner indicated that he seemed sure that he didn't have anything to worry about. The only semblance of contrition occurred when he averted his eyes as I stared at him from the witness stand when I testified. It appeared to me that this young man was certainly not going to let any conscience he might have bother him in the least for what he had done.

The trial took three days, and the verdict came rather quickly: guilty.

At least that's something in the right direction, I thought.

Following the verdict, the judge ordered a presentence investigation. I was told this process took about one month. Still concerned about the possibility (or rather, the *probability*) that Jimmy would be receiving probation instead of any real punishment, I sought out and met with the person conducting this investigation (and who would be recommending sentencing specifics to the judge).

During our conversation, this investigator commented that it was "extraordinary" that I wanted to meet with him. In fact, he said that—although it was neither unethical nor inappropriate—I was the only victim family member who ever met with him during the investigation stage of all the cases he had handled. As for myself, I was surprised that other victims of crimes did *not* seek out these investigators to give them our viewpoints and our opinions. We *should* inject information into this process to let the judicial system know how much these crimes have impacted us.

The investigator told me that he had already met with Jimmy, and that Jimmy was "very sorry" for what he did and that he "felt terrible" about what had happened. I dismissed that, explaining that Jimmy had never made a single gesture to me or my family—either directly or indirectly—to let me know that he was the slightest bit remorseful or that he even felt bad. I also pointed out that Jimmy certainly had a vested interest in convincing this investigator that he was contrite, but I had seen nothing like that coming from him. The investigator finally admitted that Jimmy could well have been insincere during their meeting.

When the time arrived for the sentencing hearing, I attended and listened as the judge ordered Jimmy to a halfway house for ninety days for evaluation and treatment of alcohol and drug abuse. Jimmy was to return to court after that period of time for final sentencing. It wasn't prison—as I had hoped—but at least it wasn't probation.

In the meantime, I continued my own efforts to find some kind of justice. I approached personnel in the state driver's license department, and they confirmed that being found guilty of killing someone on the roads and highways did result in revocation of driving privileges for one year. In addition, the supervisor I spoke with explained that in most cases there were exceptions to such revocations; offenders were often granted limited driving privileges that allowed them to drive to and from grocery stores, work, church, and so on during this revocation period. *So, even revoking driving privileges isn't absolute,* I thought.

However, during this conversation I discovered that there was an area in the law that I might be able to use. I learned that there was a process whereby *I* could have some control over Jimmy's driving privileges. I found out that if there was an outstanding judgment or financial claim against an uninsured driver (arising from damages from an at-fault accident), that person's driving license could be suspended—and *remain* suspended—for *years*, if necessary, until those financial obligations were satisfied. I was given the details of what would be necessary to do this.

At the time of the accident, I had minimal liability coverage under the uninsured motorist section of my policy (as well as medical coverage), and my insurance company paid our outstanding medical costs and Erik's funeral expenses. But my car was seven years old and had over 125,000 miles on it, so it didn't have much value (it was worth approximately $1,000 at the time of the accident). I had dropped my collision insurance coverage, and thus the insurance company did not reimburse me for the value of my car. In their investigations, the insurance company had determined that Jimmy had no financial assets, so they declined to engage in any collection action against him. He was, as they say, "judgment proof."

I thought that this was also grossly unfair; Jimmy's insolvency protected him from any type of financial responsibility for causing an accident that had killed one person and injured three others, and he had cost *others* many tens of thousands of dollars in medical bills, funeral expenses, and property damage. And he wasn't even going to be required to pay for so much as a traffic ticket!

I decided to file a lawsuit against Jimmy myself. I found a newly minted attorney who was willing to work for an hourly rate. I scraped together a retainer fee, and I had him file a civil lawsuit against Jimmy. I knew that if I sued for Erik's death (under the state's wrongful death statutes), I could easily obtain a huge judgment, but that would have been useless. With such a large judgment against him, Jimmy would likely have found enough money to file for personal bankruptcy and get out from under any such obligation. Instead, the lawsuit I filed was for only the value of my car: $1,000. I figured that this amount was small enough to make any bankruptcy filing on his part impractical. In order to defend himself against a civil lawsuit, Jimmy would have to hire his own lawyer, as he couldn't be represented by a public defender in civil court. I figured that Jimmy would likely simply ignore my lawsuit.

I was right.

Jimmy never appeared at court when this case was heard, and I easily obtained a default judgment against him. I then had this judgment filed with the appropriate office of the state driver's license department, and I was assured that Jimmy's driving privileges were now suspended until he paid what he owed under this judgment.

I had no illusion that this would actually *prevent* Jimmy from driving; after all, he had been driving without a valid license that night when he caused the accident that killed Erik. But I thought it would at least be a constant irritant to him; each time he drove a car, he'd be worried or concerned that he might be pulled over by a policeman and caught driving without privileges. He'd then either be arrested or ticketed each time (whichever the policy of the arresting police agency would be at that time).

This judgment had to be refiled periodically with the court and the driver's license bureau in order to remain effective, which I dutifully did. Over the ensuing years, Jimmy once contacted my attorney and inquired about setting up a payment schedule to satisfy the judgment, but he never followed through nor paid anything on it. I don't know how effective this was as an annoyance to Jimmy over the following years, but it brought me some satisfaction to think that he probably had been somewhat irritated by this situation year after year. In the end, I computed that it had cost me over $1,500 in legal fees to file this suit and to maintain the judgment over that time. This was more than the amount of the judgment, but I considered it money well spent.

When Jimmy returned to court following his ninety-day commitment to the halfway house, I was there again. Before the hearing started, I saw that Jimmy arrived with a child of his own; he held and played with a baby that appeared to be about three or four months old. That immediately pierced my heart. Jimmy was himself a father and was enjoying *his* child, while my child was dead—at the hands of this man.

There were several people receiving sentences that day. Jimmy was in a good mood and appeared confident. When it came to be his turn, the judge told Jimmy he was returning him to the halfway house for another ninety days.

"I've already been there," Jimmy protested.

"And I'm sending you back!" snapped the judge.

From this brief exchange, I surmised that there might have been problems during Jimmy's first stay at the halfway house; perhaps he didn't complete the treatment program, or maybe he wasn't being cooperative. It *did* mean that we were both returning to Jimmy's next sentencing hearing after ninety more days to see what would happen next. Again, it wasn't probation, but I was still hoping for at least *some* incarceration in the future.

A couple of weeks later, I heard on a radio newscast that Jimmy had "walked away" from the drug-treatment halfway house. Initially, this made me happy because I thought that Jimmy would now be charged with escape, and this meant another felony and the probability of serious jail time. But a call to the prosecutor's office quickly deflated my hopes. The person I spoke to informed me that technically Jimmy hadn't "escaped." Since he had not been officially *sentenced* to the halfway house (he was sent there for evaluation and treatment), Jimmy couldn't be charged with escape. But this action did mean, however, that Jimmy would now have a warrant issued for his arrest (so that he could be returned to court for final sentencing). This status—combined with the loss of his driving privileges—gave me at least some satisfaction to know that Jimmy would constantly live in apprehension and fear of being discovered and apprehended.

A few years later, I learned that Jimmy had finally been taken into custody and sentenced to the Utah State Prison for the zero-to-five-year term. He did not get probation as I had feared he would; that was good. But his incarceration apparently occurred only because he had angered the judge by walking away from the treatment program.

Whatever, I thought. *At least he's in prison.* Jimmy was receiving *some* punishment for what he did, and being in prison meant he wasn't in a position to hurt other people.

A little over a year after that, however, it was announced on the local television news that the Utah Supreme Court had reversed Jimmy S.'s automobile homicide conviction.

I was stunned.

I went to the State Capitol Building myself and got a copy of the decision from the court. I read it carefully. From what I could decipher from the legalese, it said that the Utah Supreme Court had decided to change the rules of the justice game. Apparently, the previous rule was that the state had to prove gross negligence on the part of an offender in order to obtain a conviction for automobile homicide. Jimmy's trial court *did* use that standard and had instructed the jury accordingly. But now, three of the five justices of the Court decided to change this rule so that *criminal* negligence would be required in all future cases (which was apparently a higher level of negligence). They thus reversed Jimmy's conviction and sent the case back to the trial court. I read that the other two justices wrote a dissenting opinion indicating that changing this rule was all good and well, but in this particular case, the higher criteria of criminal negligence *was* met by the facts, and they saw no need to reverse the lower court's conviction. Nevertheless, the three-to-two decision meant that Jimmy's conviction was reversed. A few weeks later, Jimmy was released from prison.

I again called the prosecutor's office and asked if they were going to retry the case. I mentioned that this was a felony, which likely needed to be on Jimmy's record (so that it can be considered when he commits other crimes in the future). I was told that they would not retry the case. One of the reasons that the new assistant prosecutor gave me was that "it wasn't a violent crime."

That comment shocked me: *Killing someone wasn't a violent crime?*

"It was pretty violent at the time," I replied. "There was a lot of blood and damage there, and my son had been killed. Isn't that violent?"

Regardless of what I had to say, I was told that their office was not going to devote any more of their resources to this case. It was over and finished as far as they were concerned.

I was deeply troubled by this turn of events. Jimmy's record would now be cleared of this conviction, and it felt like the justice system was telling me that all of this really didn't happen—that nothing was wrong.

But something *was* wrong, *terribly* wrong. A beautiful child had been killed, and the societal values and the government justice system didn't seem to be able to do much about it or to try to prevent this from happening again and again to others.

I wanted to scream out to everyone what an insane world we lived in: people get drunk and drive cars around, and society seemed to accept this behavior. DUI convictions were not taken seriously, and offenders reoffended multiple times with little concern of any substantial punishment. I saw that people killed other people with their cars while they were drunk (tens of thousands of innocent people lose their lives every year due to drunk drivers in the United States alone), and—at least in Utah—they usually received *probation.* I also saw that when there *were* convictions, the courts could change the rules of the game at any time and reverse some of those convictions.

Like many other family members of those who have died tragic, senseless deaths, I wanted to change things; I wanted to try to do something to prevent such insanity from continuing—to try to save another family, another parent, from going through the horror and pain that I was going through.

I wanted to join or create an advocacy group to lobby for changes that would make a difference, to change society's apparent lackadaisical attitude about drunk driving. I wanted to help change the laws to stiffen penalties (including mandatory jail time) for those who drive drunk and to lower the legal BAC level to 0.08. I wanted automobile homicide to be treated as a *serious* crime (at *least* as a second-degree felony), because the consequences of these offenses were as devastating as crimes committed with guns or other weapons.

At that period of my life, I was living a hand-to-mouth existence; my expenses and bills were such that I barely made ends meet each month. I didn't have the funds or the knowledge to mount a publicity campaign to get my message out (this was many years before the Internet was developed). Although I did talk with some politicians and government bureaucrats about these issues on a one-on-one basis when the occasion and situation merited it, I didn't have the means or opportunity to reach a wide or influential audience. I couldn't tell other people what was happening in order to recruit others to help lobby for changes. I felt impotent in being able to do anything meaningful for society.

Years later, I saw that another parent had tragically gone through what I had experienced, and this person *was* able to do something on a national level. Candace "Candy" Lightner formed Mothers Against Drunk Driving (MADD), which has been a driving force to change laws and attitudes regarding drunk driving. This is exactly what I wanted to do when this happened to me, but I didn't have the knowledge, connections, or resources to effectively do anything meaningful.

After the reversal of Jimmy's conviction, I continued to maintain my personal civil judgment against him, thus denying him the right to have a legal driver's license. I thought it was the *least* I could do, and I often felt disappointed that that was *all* that I did.

A few years later, when I was working in central Utah, I received a telephone call from my middle brother.

"Have you seen today's newspaper?" he asked.

"Why? What's up?" I responded.

"Jimmy S. is dead. It says he was killed by someone at a street party yesterday."

I quickly purchased a newspaper and found the short news item: There had been a street party in Salt Lake City, and an argument had broken out between two people. One was shot in the back, who later died. The perpetrator and other party participants left the scene. Authorities said that the victim had no identification on him, but they were able to ascertain his name through his fingerprints. It was also reported that authorities found that the victim had some unnamed illicit drugs sewn into the lining of his jacket.

My first thought was that it was good that I had an alibi; I was living three hours away by car from Salt Lake, and I could account for all of my movements that day. My second thought was that I felt *relieved*. Justice—or karma—had finally been dealt to the person who killed my son. I knew it was supposed to be an appalling thing to take satisfaction in another's misfortune—especially their death—but that's what I felt. I was relieved that this person no longer walked the Earth, no longer breathed air or ate food, no longer enjoyed life. Jimmy had deprived Erik of all the joys of life and *his* future, and now Jimmy was gone as well.

The following day, I read the obituary that was printed, and I actually made the trip up to Salt Lake City on the day of Jimmy's funeral. I arrived at the cemetery after whatever graveside ceremony had taken place and I saw that Jimmy's concrete vault had been lowered into the open grave. After a few minutes, the cemetery workers arrived and started filling it in. I remained there and watched.

At that point, I felt a sense of closure—a partial conclusion to this situation. The person who was responsible for the death of my son was gone, and my anger receded considerably.

I don't know if many professional counselors would say that my anger was therapeutic—rather than detrimental—but I felt that it had actually *helped* me over those few years. My anger helped focus me and assisted in giving me a path to pursue; it gave me a goal: justice. But now I had reached the end of that road.

I felt free to pursue the rest of my life.

Thirteen

Starting Over

Every end is a new beginning.
—*Proverb*

In the immediate aftermath of Erik's death, I felt that my core identity had been lost; I didn't know who or what I was anymore. I had been a husband, but I destroyed that role myself through my own decisions and actions by getting divorced. Most importantly, however, I had also been a *father*—a role and identity which I had come to love and treasure above all else. But after Erik died, I was technically no longer a father. If I had no children, how could I still be called a father? The loss of that status was very painful to me.

I remember wondering, *What should I do when someone asks me if I have any children? What do I say?* If I said I had no children, then that would have seemed like I was denying Erik's existence—as if he never lived—and I *couldn't* do that; he had been such a major part of my life. If I answered, "I have one child, a son," then what should I say when the usual follow-up question was asked, "And how old is he?" I saw that such an innocent and normal conversation starter could quickly enter the realm of "too much information." Did I really want to go into details that are painful to me as well as likely to cause the other person to become uncomfortable or uneasy? Should I just reply, "Two," and try to change the subject? This would be somewhat dishonest, since I was giving the impression that I had a two-year-old son running around at home. Or should I say, "He was two years old when he died," and then try to deal with the shocked response that was certain to come from the other person? I came up with no set plan or procedure; I decided to play each conversation by ear, and I gave responses that seemed to match the particular situations and settings in which such questions occurred.

Having lost the identities of husband—and especially father—I embarked on a foolhardy mission to try to immediately rectify that situation. I felt I *needed* to become an actual father again—*soon*. At that point, I knew that if human cloning had been even an extremely remote possibility, I would have moved heaven and Earth to make such a thing happen; I would have gone into lifelong debt, borne any hardships, done anything at all. I just wanted my son alive again. I wanted my little boy back with me. Given the impossibility of such an action, I examined other ways that I might be able to reconstruct my identity and my life.

I first thought about getting back together with Janet and having another baby with her. Subconsciously, I believe I wanted to *recreate* Erik—to somehow bring him back to us. When I broached the subject of us getting back together and having another child, Janet wisely declined.

The next step I took was to try to establish a relationship with another woman—*any* woman—to try to create a family again, *quickly*. I had heard the advice (and warnings) from others who had been divorced that a person should wait at least a year before engaging in another serious relationship. I *couldn't* wait that long; at that time, waiting one year before even *beginning* to see someone new seemed to be an eternity. Instead, I immediately started looking for someone to marry. I seriously believed that my very *sanity* depended upon this, that I needed to establish myself in a family situation again, to become a father again.

Living in Salt Lake City, I found myself in a somewhat unusual situation. Most of the people in that city (and the state of Utah) were Mormons. Although I was no longer engaged in that church, I knew all about it, and I knew how they lived and what their professed values were. One of the main traditions of the Mormon Church is that its adult members should be married and that they should have children as soon as possible after marriage.

The LDS Church hierarchy at that time set up organizational structures and processes to facilitate these goals. One such structure was the establishment of specific congregations (or *wards*, as they called them) that were restricted to unmarried members between eighteen and thirty years of age. Ordinarily, Mormon congregations consisted of *all* of their members who lived in a specific geographical location—young and old alike. But the rationale for grouping only young, single adults together was to put many such people into close proximity with each other so that they could interact, find partners, and get married. Once married, these young adults were then no longer allowed to be part of these singles' wards and were required to attend the traditional, multigenerational family wards instead.

At that point in my life, I was single (divorced), I was twenty-eight years old, and I *desperately* wanted to have a family again—and *children*. I believed that I could successfully exist within the Mormon organization if I only had a wife with whom I was compatible and who wanted children. Although I was open to any and all possibilities—from any religion, nonreligion, or walk of life—my search for a future wife was expanded to possibly include someone from the Mormon Church, and I started to attend their local singles' ward.

Approximately one month after Erik died, I started my new job as a special education resource room teacher at one of the larger elementary schools in the city. There were several newly-minted teachers working at that building, including two young women who lived in another apartment complex that was adjacent to the one where I lived. Soon, the three of us were carpooling back and forth to work. After several weeks, I expressed interest in one of these teachers, and we dated for a while. An engagement occurred shortly thereafter. However, this relationship soon ended (as could well be expected), since I was still an emotional wreck.

My reaction after this latest breakup, however, was quite severe. At that point, I felt like I was at the end of my rope; I couldn't take any more of the stress and difficulties in my life. I had just gone through one *horrible* year. During the previous twelve months, I had a marriage that failed, Janet had moved Erik two states away from me, I had a brief relationship in Idaho that also failed, I left my job in Idaho and moved to Utah to start new employment, my beautiful, precious little son was killed, I had an ongoing struggle trying to get the Utah justice system to function, and now another failed relationship. Each of these separate events was extremely stressful and difficult on its own, but to have *all* these terrible events unloaded on me within this relatively short time period was overwhelming. I felt like I was in a deep hole, with life constantly shoveling dirt and rocks down onto me, and I had no way to climb out; I felt like I was being emotionally and psychologically suffocated.

The feelings of worthlessness that I had lived with as a child then returned, and they combined with all of the stressors, problems, and grief that I was now experiencing.

At that point, I began to have suicidal thoughts; I felt that I needed to leave this world—I couldn't live like that anymore. I began to make some comments, and I left a few clues concerning my state of mind. I remember one day when a colleague (a teaching assistant) at my new school was trying to buoy me up by telling me that I needed to persevere through my hardships. She knew that I had lost my child shortly before school started and that my relationship with another teacher at that same school building had just gone south. She told me, "Well, life must go on."

"Not necessarily," I replied.

I was told later by another coworker that my response really frightened this woman, and I regretted causing her any alarm or worry.

It was at this time when one of the lay leaders of the local Mormon ward found out about my suicidal comments. He said, "You know, if you kill yourself, you'll never be able to see your son again in the afterlife."

That statement angered me. I told him, "You have no right and no authority to decide or to tell me whether or not I'll see Erik again. You never met him; you never knew him. You don't know what relationship we had with each other. We had a love between us that will *never* end, and *however* I die, I *will* be with him again." He didn't respond.

After a few days, the suicidal thoughts diminished, and I eventually made it through that dark period. Part of what changed in me was that I adopted a different thought process concerning one of my main issues. Instead of viewing each passing day as another day that I was getting farther and farther away from Erik, I now viewed each day that I lived as another day I was coming closer to my own natural death, and with that death, the opportunity to see and be with Erik again.

After this last breakup, I slowed down. I decided that desperation was not a good basis for a potential relationship. I backed off from the obsession that I *had* to get married, that I *had* to have children and a family again *immediately*. I continued to attend the Mormon Church's local singles' ward, and I participated in their activities. But this time I viewed this as a social outlet—as a way to interact with different people and to possibly develop some friendships. The problem with this approach, however, was that there was a sense of competitiveness that permeated the entire singles' ward culture, since most people were there expressly to meet, get engaged, and get married. Everyone was competing for the most desirable prizes.

After some months, I did notice one young woman, Mary, in some of the church activity groups in which I sometimes participated (called "Home Evening" groups). She was a year younger than I was, and she had a portion of that outgoing, social personality that I had seen in the two girls I had dated briefly when I was a teenager. By this time, however, my own personality had reverted back nearly to the same point when *I* was a teenager: shy, insecure, and socially inept with a low self-image and poor sense of self-worth.

I eventually asked Mary out, and we started dating. Again, I was surprised to find someone who was willing to go on more than one or two dates with me. I didn't push things, however, as I wanted any possible relationship try to evolve on its own. Over the following months, we became closer, and a more serious relationship developed. During this period, however, I had become nonassertive to the point that it was *Mary* who had to finally ask me if I thought we should get married. I was surprised when she asked because Mary appeared to be the quintessential social person, trying to please everyone, while I was the opposite: a social dullard. It also seemed like everyone around us (including my own family) was constantly telling me—and continued to remind me—as to what a "special" person Mary was and that I was very lucky to have someone like her in my life. In fact, I got the definite impression that some people couldn't understand how or why a wonderful person like Mary would (or could) be romantically interested in someone such as me. I also wondered why she would be interested in me, since my own sense of self-worth had regressed back to the point where I didn't believe I was worthy of anything that might be good in my life.

Mary was a charmer. My immediate family seemed to be especially taken with her. On those occasions when I stopped by or visited my parents' house *without* Mary in tow, they appeared to be disappointed and their first questions were, "Where's Mary? Why isn't she with you?" It seemed to me that my parents preferred Mary's company to mine.

I thought that it was quite remarkable—extraordinary, really—that in Mary I had *really* beaten the odds: out of the literally *billions* of people on this Earth, I had found the only other person who was actually willing to have a relationship (and sex) with me! If I was in Las Vegas, I thought I could've made a fortune many times over with this kind of luck.

Mary shared some of my same wishes and objectives; she also wanted to be part of a family unit, and she wanted to have children. These were *my* goals, as well.

During our engagement, I thought about some early warning signs I had witnessed in our relationship so far, but I generally dismissed them. Mary was more involved with and dedicated to the Mormon church than I was, but I thought that we were flexible enough so that this wouldn't be a large impediment. I also witnessed a strange dependency relationship between Mary and her parents (particularly her mother). Nevertheless, I thought that these—and other issues—were manageable and wouldn't present any major problems that couldn't be dealt with successfully the future. After all, we were in love!

Unfortunately, I found out later that this would not be true.

Fourteen

A New Family

Call it a clan, call it a network, call it a tribe.
Whatever you call it, whoever you are, you need one.
—*Jane Howard*

Mary and I were married after an engagement of several
months. My second son (and Mary's first child), Karl, was
born seventeen months after our wedding. This was just over
three years and eight months after Erik died. My dreams of
having a family—and becoming a father again—were finally
coming true.

In the short interim between our marriage and Karl's
birth, we had moved a couple of times and we ended up back
in southern Idaho. Consequently, Karl was born in the same
hospital where Erik was born. And—just as Erik's birth process
had complications—Karl's birth came with its own problems.
Within a few hours of his birth, the doctor told me that my new
son had some problem with his lungs because he had aspirated
something that wasn't supposed to be there. I was told that
Karl needed to be taken to a larger hospital that was about
fifteen miles away, which had a neonatal intensive care unit

(NICU) that could give better care for him. When I asked if he would be taken there by ambulance, I was told it would be quicker for me to transport him myself. The doctor said that they would call the other hospital to tell them we were coming. Mary's mother was staying with us at the time, so she got in the backseat with Karl while I drove—rather quickly, I might add.

When we arrived at the larger hospital, I entered through the emergency room door holding Karl in my arms, and I explained my situation. They directed me straight to the hospital's NICU on another floor. Upon locating this unit, I spoke with the nurse on duty and again explained why I was there. If anyone *had* called from the original hospital, this nurse was certainly unaware of it and didn't know what was happening. However, things were quickly straightened out and the nurse then took baby Karl from my arms. I asked what was going to happen with him and what they were going to do to him.

"Don't worry. He'll be all right," she said somewhat dismissively as she started to walk away with my newborn son.

At that moment, it felt like a switch was flipped in my brain. My reaction was immediate; my anxiety level skyrocketed.

"No!" I said, forcefully, shaking my head. "No!" I took a deep breath and added, "The last time someone said that to me—'He'll be all right'—it was about my first son, three years ago. And then the next time I saw him, he was dead. So... *please*...tell me what you're going to do with him."

After a brief pause, the nurse changed her attitude and took me seriously. She clearly explained their procedures to me, including examination and assessment, along with possible treatment options, and so forth. This only took a couple of minutes. At the end, I thanked her. I felt my stress level recede significantly.

It wasn't until that moment when the nurse uttered those words, *Don't worry; he'll be all right,* that I realized that this was one of the triggers of my PTSD (post-traumatic stress disorder), a condition I had developed after the traffic accident in which Erik had died.

I had experienced other triggering events of PTSD previously. The most obvious occurred whenever I found myself driving on a wide, city street on a warm summer evening, approaching a dedicated left turn lane (especially when my car was going to be the first one in line to turn left). These conditions mirrored the circumstances of that dreadful night when Erik was killed, and whenever they occurred my hands got sweaty, my heart raced, and my breathing became quick and shallow. My anxiety level would go through the roof. After this happened a couple of times, I learned to keep away from these conditions at all cost. I avoided driving on warm, clear summer evenings. Whenever I saw that my car was going to be first in line of a separate left turn lane, I would instead drive through that intersection and go around the next block to avoid repeating these conditions.

It has taken many years for the anxiety associated with my PTSD triggers to lessen to the degree that it does not significantly impact my daily functioning. When I am currently exposed to these situations or those words, I don't become overly stressed, but I am aware of—and I do remember— the circumstances that initiated these anxieties in the first place.

After about three days, Karl and his mother were discharged from their respective hospitals. Both were doing fine.

However, I did have some conflicting feelings surrounding Karl's arrival. Karl was my son, and he was another beautiful boy. I loved him, and I was *very* happy that he came to us. But at the same time, I was somewhat afraid. I was afraid of loving him *too* much, as I had probably done with Erik. Erik had become my whole life, and I had come to depend on him for my own happiness. When Erik died, my life shattered, and the pain was unbearable. What if the same thing should happen to Karl? What if *he* died? If I let myself become as emotionally attached to Karl as I had been to Erik, could I survive if another tragedy happened to *him*? I *hated* the fact that these feelings were bubbling just below the surface, waiting to spring out whenever I let my guard down.

I eventually came to realize that my relationship with Erik was—on some level—likely an unhealthy one for me and probably quite unfair to Erik. When he was alive, I was relying on Erik to fulfill my own hopes and dreams and to provide me with happiness. He was a precious and beautiful little child—he didn't need that kind of responsibility; it wasn't his obligation to make me happy.

Of course, I loved Karl very much and I did everything with him as I had done with Erik; I played with him, talked to him, tickled him, changed him, and fed him (when I could, because Mary chose to breastfeed our children). But I didn't assign Karl the responsibility of making me happy; he was, after all, a baby. My goals with Karl—which were the same goals that I had with all my subsequent children—were to make sure that he knew that he was loved and wanted. My goals included assurances that my children were healthy, well fed, and cared for and, to the best of my ability, that they were *happy*.

Fifteen months after Karl was born, my first daughter, Marit, arrived. Her birth was quick, and without complications. Karl now had a little sister to dote on, and he enjoyed her very much. Later on, these two became inseparable, laughing and playing and talking with each other, often until the late hours of the night.

When Karl approached his second birthday, however, I became aware of a heightened anxiety level on my part. As a young child, Karl's behavior was, in many ways, similar to Erik at that age. What concerned me—no, what *frightened* me—was the idea in my head that something might happen to him, just as it had happened to Erik. I was terrified of this possibility. Also, because of what had happened to Erik, I became extremely vigilant about his (and my other children's) safety, whether at home or out in the community. Throughout their childhood and teen years, car seats were installed, safety products were fitted in our house, bicycle helmets and life vests were purchased, and I carefully watched and monitored them both at home and out in the community. I absolutely did not want *any* harm to come to *any* of them.

Karl turned two, and I became more concerned and nervous for him. As the following days and weeks crept by, my anxiety increased. By the time Karl was two years and two months old (the age at which Erik had died), I felt constantly stressed and on guard. This hypervigilance gradually abated over the following months and years as Karl passed that dreaded benchmark.

Later, Peder arrived, and Karl and Marit both had a little brother to take care of—until he got older and could run and play with his older siblings.

Then came Lisbeth. I remember coming home from the hospital after Lisbeth's birth and announcing to my children that they now had a little sister. Five-year-old Marit was particularly happy upon hearing that news, and she gave a little fist pump, exclaiming, "Yes!"

Finally, Gunnar Roy came, and my new family was complete (at that point, Mary had a tubal ligation procedure after this final birth).

I did continue one of the traditions I had started with Erik: I gave each of my children a Norwegian name so that they could be aware of (and reminded of) that part of their heritage. I tried to pick out names that would be acceptable both in the United States and in Norway. However, given the problems I had with my own name when I was growing up, one might wonder why I would inflict that name on one of my children. We tried to mitigate any negative effects of this name by starting out with the English pronunciation of "Gunner" instead of trying to maintain the Norwegian pronunciation. This strategy has seemed to work over the years, as my youngest son has not reported any undue teasing or problems with his name.

With each of these children, my love and attachment grew. I *loved* playing with my children, taking care of them, and just *being* with them whenever I could.

I was a father again, and I had a family again. I had accomplished what I had set out to do. We were all traveling together on that problem-filled road of adventure called *life*.

Fifteen

Stress

L ife has its problems, of course, and many might say that life is a seemingly endless chain of problems, one following the other (and often overlapping each other). And with each problem comes a heightened degree of stress and anxiety (until the problem is solved or dealt with effectively). Being a husband and the father of five children produced an ample quantity of these stress-inducing problems.

Throughout my working career, one of my largest fears— and a huge source of stress—was of the possibility of losing my job and thereby losing my ability to financially support my family. How could I feed or clothe my family if I didn't have an income? Where would we live? I was afraid that if I missed a single rent or mortgage payment, we would immediately be homeless and on the road to starvation. That was an unthinkable possibility in my mind—something I didn't even want to imagine—but it was a very real fear.

This obsessive concern on my part did have some basis in reality. When I began my professional career as a special education teacher, I was initially hired to work in a small school district in eastern Idaho. This was before Erik was born, so it was only me and Janet (my first wife) at that time. However, I was only employed in that position for two years; the district superintendent declined to rehire me for the third year (he told me he was letting me go so that I would not be eligible for tenured employment status). Without tenure, I was an "at will" employee, and as such, the district was under no obligation to offer me a position for the third year, and they were also not obligated to give me any reason or explanation for letting me go. I'd had some problems during my first year in that district, but the second year went much better, and I thought everything had been settled. But apparently not. In any event, I was left looking for another job without a positive recommendation from my previous employer. That turned out to be a very difficult task.

Even though there were special education teaching positions available with other school districts in the area, they were suddenly closed to me when my previous school superintendent was contacted. I didn't know what this man was saying to potential employers, but it was quite effective in eliminating me from consideration.

I eventually did find a teaching position in northern Idaho with a private agency that contracted special education programs and services for teenage clients through the state health and welfare department (I later discovered that the supervisor for this program had *not* contacted my previous employer before hiring me). This job was part of a new start-up program, and at the time I was hired, I was told that it would be an ongoing program that was projected to continue into the foreseeable future.

So, Janet and I paid a trucking company to move our trailer house nearly five hundred miles to our new location, and I had to take out a loan from a bank to cover the moving costs. But this was my second chance to continue in my trained career, and I did what I had to do so we could keep living.

As fate would have it, however, four units of this new program were discontinued after that initial year, and mine was one of them. I was out of work again. At that point, I thought that I might be in the wrong field of work entirely, and I seriously considered changing professions.

Since my unemployment was the result of a "reduction in force" (due to discontinuing those four units and laying off the eight employees associated with them), I went to the state employment office to apply for temporary unemployment benefits until I found other work. That's when I discovered that school teachers were (and are) not eligible for unemployment benefits in Idaho. I was told that teachers work on set, limited period contracts (one year at a time), and are thus not actually considered ongoing, permanent employees. I pointed out that I was laid off from a private agency and not from a public school system, but I was told that didn't matter; due to the fact that my job title was "teacher" and that I had a contract that had definite starting and ending dates, I was not a permanent employee and not eligible for unemployment compensation under any circumstances.

This caused even more long-term stress and anxiety in me. This meant that as long as I remained in this profession, I was not offered the same level or type of temporary "safety net" that other workers could count on in emergencies.

That summer, I started taking business, accounting, and computer science classes from a college just over the border with Washington. I was seriously considering a different career. In the meantime, however, I continued to look for possible employment in the field of education (although I thought my chances of finding a third position after losing two previous positions in only three years were rather slim).

I eventually *did* find another teaching position, but it was in southern Idaho. That meant another move and another bank loan to pay for the 560-mile trip with our trailer house again (the first loan having just been paid off).

Upon obtaining another teaching position, I did not continue to pursue any new professional training and I remained in the education field for the remainder of my working career. I sometimes wonder what new path my life might have taken if I had remained in north Idaho and completed a business and/or computer science curriculum. But I needed money— some kind of income—to live on, and so I took work wherever I could find it.

These early experiences, however, did instill into my mind the perception that my continued employment was not a permanent proposition, that I could lose my job at *any* time for *any* reason (or for possibly *no* reason at all, if I was untenured).

I sometimes thought that part of my problem might be that I was not really an integral component of the communities in which I was working. By that, I mean that I wasn't born and raised in the community—I was one of the outsiders who came in to take a job and who would likely leave and move on to other jobs and other places (for whatever reason) in the future. I envied those teachers and other workers who were integral parts of their communities, who grew up, went to school, and took positions within the local school system or for private companies, and who stayed in these positions for several decades (until their retirement). I knew that I could *never* be in such a situation. The city where I was born—and where my ancestors came from—was in a completely different country on another continent. To me, this was further confirmation that it might have been better if we had remained in Norway and not moved to the United States. In Norway, we would have been connected to the community where our family name had been well known for centuries. I would've loved to have had roots in *one* location rather than to have jumped around from place to place, trying to gain a foothold in what seemed to be shifting sand.

This basic uncertainty in employment and potential financial insecurity led me to make several decisions that affected me and my family for many years to come. Just as many financial counselors often do in advising their clients to diversify their stock portfolios, I decided that I needed to try to diversify my *income*. I was terrified of relying on one employer—essentially *one* person, such as a school district superintendent—for my total economic security and my future. Also, my experience during the previous three years was that I was living paycheck to paycheck; I had little to no excess income each month above my expenses, and I would often have to pay for unexpected or emergency expenses with credit cards (thus going even deeper into debt). So, I decided I needed to diversify my income somehow.

By the time Janet and I had moved to southern Idaho, I decided to look for part-time work to supplement my teacher salary. I soon found a position as a security guard for a company that provided services to a local manufacturing plant. I worked there between three and four shifts a week, and this helped alleviate some of the financial stress and pressure that I was experiencing. The following year, people from the school district's administration approached me and asked if I would also like to drive a short school bus route for a small additional income. I accepted.

Ever since I obtained that first part-time job, I have *always* worked at two, three, and sometimes even four jobs at one time during my working career. This continued until my retirement.

The fear of losing my employment drove me to take these additional jobs, but these endeavors came at their own substantial costs, as well. Putting in time at these extra jobs significantly limited the time I had available to spend with my children.

Another part of the driving force that I experienced was the strong aversion of being dependent on others for my income (that is, being an *employee*). Again, this was an extension of my desire to be free from the whims and desires of others who had financial control over my very life and existence. Other people were in charge of whether or not my family and I were going to be able to continue to live in our house, to buy gas for the car, to make the payments for the car, to be able to go to a doctor when needed, or to buy food and groceries in order to even *exist*. The stress of that possibility hung around my neck like a chain and anchor. This constant anxiety also led me to make other financial decisions that ended quite badly and were ultimately counterproductive.

Over the years, I engaged in a number of moneymaking plans in my attempt to become financially independent. The point of many of these efforts was to start my own business, beginning part time, with the hope of gaining enough momentum and profit to enable me to eventually *stop* being an employee. These business attempts included trying to lease personal computers to schools (at a time when computers first appeared on the market), opening a copy and print shop, buying a candy vending machine route, purchasing and placing several coin-operated laundry machines in various locations, and at one point I even considered opening my own technical school. I once purchased a majority stake in an ongoing appliance sales and service retail store, and—over the years—I also bought three very old houses to use as rental properties (each of which I ended up living in and having to remodel).

Each and every one of these schemes suffered from the same fatal flaws: I had no coherent, long-term business plan and I lacked the capital to viably start and maintain these schemes. I invested *borrowed* money into all of these enterprises, and I tried to maintain these businesses by investing additional money from my already-stretched monthly paychecks. Often, I also borrowed more and more (from credit card accounts) to try to keep these fledgling ventures afloat. I was hoping that the businesses that I was trying to establish would somehow take off and start me on the road to financial independence.

It never happened.

Instead, each of these enterprises cost *more* to operate than any income I received from them. The longer I was trying to run them, the more I was getting myself deeper and deeper into debt. As a result, I found myself more and more dependent on that one source of income that I was trying to rid myself from: being an employee at the mercy of others. Without the essential, required preparation (that is, having a business plan and sufficient *cash* capital to get a business off the ground), my efforts were in fact quite counterproductive— I was making everything *much* worse. The constant stress and anxiety of always living on the edge of financial ruin took a toll on me and my relationships with others. Also, with each business closure, I was reinforcing that part of my self-concept that I had first learned when I was quite young and that I always lived with: I was a failure and a disappointment.

Another major stressor that I experienced after my second marriage was the influence of the LDS Church on me, my family, and my relationship with my wife, Mary.

As I've mentioned previously, I returned to the Mormon Church as part of my desperate efforts to find a wife, have other children, and establish a family. I knew about the Mormon beliefs and practices, and I had decided I could accept those aspects of the church that I saw as valuable, and I thought that I could disregard or ignore those parts of the church that I found to be bizarre and odd.

What I wanted was a happy and functional family—to enjoy and raise children with love and care. This was something I did not have in my own childhood, but I wanted it for *my* children. To me, the purpose of religion was to offer assistance in living a good life and to provide guidance when needed. What I did *not* want was to experience the religious absurdities and extremes that permeated my life as a child and teenager. In short, I had decided I could be a "cafeteria" Mormon, valuing those things I found to be positive, while discarding (or ignoring) those parts that were irrelevant or harmful.

When I met and married Mary, I thought I had found a somewhat kindred spirit. I knew that she was more "Mormony" than I was, but I didn't think that she was—or would be—obsessed with and completely controlled by the church. After all, Mary had often behaved in ways that were not strictly in line with the current church teachings. When we were dating, the Mormon Church leader (commonly called the prophet and/or church president) was a man named Spencer W. Kimball. Kimball was famous for his strict moral pronouncements and guidance. He advised, "Kissing has been prostituted and has degenerated to develop and express lust instead of affection, honor, and admiration. To kiss in casual dating is asking for trouble" (from the book, *Teachings of Spencer W. Kimball*). Kimball famously advised couples to experience their first kiss together as the kiss they share across the temple altar on the day that they are married.

Mary certainly didn't follow *that* advice, nor did she follow the admonition to never indulge in other disallowed behaviors. I therefore thought that she shared a reasonable approach to religion in general, and the Mormon Church in particular.

I was wrong.

Shortly after we were married, it became apparent that Mary's views concerning church matters and issues became more and more controlling and intrusive in her (and our) everyday activities. The changes weren't sudden; they crept slowly into our lives.

An example of the mind-set that the church should be allowed to control its members was demonstrated in a brief conversation I had with another young Mormon woman who carpooled with me the first year I lived and worked in Salt Lake City after Erik had died. This woman had been dating a man rather seriously, and one morning she shared with us a card she had just received from her boyfriend (he had sent it along with a bouquet of flowers).

It read, "Next to the gospel, you're the most important thing in my life."

I was surprised at this sentiment. "Aren't *you* supposed to be the most important thing in his life?" I asked.

"Oh no," she replied. "I agree with him. The gospel *is* the most important thing in our lives, and I'm certainly happy to be in second place to *that!*"

In my mind, my children and my family came first, and any church-related jobs—also referred to as "callings"—took a backseat. This attitude was based on my opinion that the purpose of religion was to supplement and add to life, not take it over. However, there are people who believe that religion *is* the primary purpose of life. Such people spend their time serving and obeying their church leaders and put *church* first in their lives. They believe that religion is the primary purpose of existence.

Through her actions, I saw that Mary developed into a member of this second group; the church trumped all else.

Taking care of babies and raising children is a full-time job that I believe should take precedence over virtually everything else. Children need their parents' time and attention. When we give other tasks priority over our childcare responsibilities, our children suffer. As parents, we experience additional stress and anxiety when we try to do too much with not enough time.

Mary accepted every voluntary position that was asked of her by the church. Included with these positions was the job to serve as a Visiting Teacher. This position involves women, working in pairs, to visit perhaps four or five other women members in their homes on a monthly basis. Besides checking on the temporal and spiritual status of these female members, the Visiting Teachers also impart a religious or inspirational message to their assigned contacts during each visit. As a very social person, Mary excelled in this role and became a consummate Visiting Teacher. She had a natural way of saying those things that encouraged others to open up and talk, and she knew how to keep a conversation going. These abilities created a situation where Mary and her companion would easily spend an hour or more with each and every one of their assigned contacts, whereas other Visiting Teacher teams might spend fifteen or twenty minutes for each visit.

This would normally be fine with me (and it was all right before our children were born), but the fact was that we had small children—well, a *number* of small children—that needed care and attention. It was my position that our children had a priority claim on our time. It was Mary's belief that church duties, jobs, and callings took precedence.

There were many occasions when I would come home from one of my jobs to find Mary gone and all of our children alone in the house, often running wild, chasing each other, and sometimes getting into fights or causing damage. Mary would eventually return, but we never knew when she would appear; it could be five minutes after I arrived, or it could be over an hour or more later. Virtually every time this occurred, I found that Mary was gone because she was engaged in her church duties, usually as a Visiting Teacher.

I tried to work with Mary to alleviate this situation. I asked her to schedule her Visiting Teacher appointments on those days and times throughout the month when I would be home. She replied that sometimes these times were inconvenient to either her assigned contacts or her Visiting Teaching partner, or that these people were unavailable at those times. I then suggested that she could perhaps tell me—a few days ahead of time—when she planned on being gone for her appointments, and I would try to rearrange my schedule to be home to watch the children. If that didn't work, we could make plans for someone else to supervise the children while she was gone. Mary would not give me any such schedule and said that the opportunity to catch someone at home would often arise without much prior notice, and she needed to take advantage of such openings whenever they came. This basically boiled down to a fundamental difference of opinions: I viewed leaving small children home alone, unattended, as a major problem (and potentially dangerous). Mary thought this was an acceptable practice, mainly because she believed she was engaged in "doing the Lord's work," as they say, when she was completing her Visiting Teaching (or other church assignments).

As our children got older, I started the practice of occasionally going to the movies together or going out to get something to eat as a family. I enjoyed these times together. When our children began to develop their own tastes and preferences in the types of movies they liked to see, I adapted our movie-going experiences to accommodate these differing tastes. Instead of taking everyone out to every movie that someone wanted to see, I would take only those children—who were interested—to a particular movie, and the other children would spend that time with their mother. Perhaps they would see a different movie, engage in some other activity, or they might remain home. The children chose for themselves who would go to the movies and who would not, and each of them spent more individualized time with a parent during these movie and activity nights.

On one such occasion, when Marit was a young teenager, she was interested in seeing a particular movie that was just coming out. Whenever possible, we would try to attend the opening night of the film that we wanted to see, with our arrangements being made—and announced—a couple of weeks ahead of the show's premier. When Marit and I were walking out the door on the appointed Friday evening to go to her movie (she was the only one of the children who wanted to see that particular show), Mary intervened. She said that Marit couldn't go. Mary unexpectedly announced that Marit needed to attend a local Young Women's activity that was scheduled for that same evening (the Young Women is one of the Mormon Church youth groups that hold different faith-building events—called activities—once a month). This was the first I had heard about any such activity or event. At that point, I objected. I said that my evening with Marit was planned well ahead of time and that this was one of our traditions in our home. Mary insisted that Marit needed to support the Young Women's group with her attendance because she was one of the three girls who were designated as part of the "presidency" (leaders) of this group. I resented this additional intrusion into our family time, and I told Mary that the church doesn't seem very "family oriented" when their activities interfere with our family time. Mary then became quite serious, looked directly at me, and said that I must be "insane" to have made such a comment. Marit went to the Young Women's activity that evening instead of the movie.

The next day, I discovered that the all-important activity the previous evening consisted of this Young Women's group of girls being driven by their adult leader to some person's house (I don't remember whose house it was), whereupon they all participated in toilet-papering the house and yard. They did it as a *joke*.

I was incensed. *This* was the faith-building activity that was so important that it cost me my special evening with Marit? *This* was part of doing the Lord's work? I took Marit to the house that they had visited, and I had her remove much of the toilet paper that had been strewn in the yard, bushes, and tree. I would certainly not have wanted to have someone do this to *my* house, and I didn't want Marit to think that it was all right to do this to anyone else's house.

Later, I complained to the adult leader of that Young Women's group (who had organized the toilet-papering activity), and I told her that I thought this was inappropriate and certainly not something that should be taught as a church activity. Another parent of a girl in that same group who was also present agreed with me. The leader just laughed it off and said that it was something that "everybody did." Several weeks later, the three top leaders (the bishopric) of our ward were visiting us at our house. I expressed my displeasure of this activity to these men as well, and I commented that some homeowners might call the police when this happens, since it could be construed as vandalism (or at least trespassing). These church leaders laughed at me too. I suppose the community values and behavioral customs that came with my urban upbringing were somewhat different from those in this rural Idaho town.

The issue of the ward callings caused other problems for me and our relationship. At one point, I was called (assigned) to be a teacher for teenage Sunday school class (boys who were fourteen or fifteen years old). They were a very rowdy and disrespectful group, as are many teenagers at that age. It was an extremely difficult assignment, and at that time I was also working at both full-time and part-time jobs, and going to graduate school for my master's degree. Life was tremendously stressful.

After quite a long time of trying to balance my life and to cope with everyday living, I had a wonderful opportunity to attend a six-week program at the University of Oslo International Summer School. This was something that I had dreamed about doing for many years. Fortunately, I applied for and had received a scholarship that paid for a large part of the expense. I also obtained approval to apply one of the classes that I was going to take from this summer program to my master's degree requirements. Everything just seemed to fall into place to allow me to follow this dream.

After weeks of arrangements, followed by long flights and airport connections, I finally arrived in Norway. Since I was going to be gone for those six weeks, the local ward leaders in Idaho had to find someone else to teach that problematic Sunday school class. I was relieved, at least for those few weeks.

During my first couple of weeks in Norway, I thought a lot about my situation with the church back home, and I made what I thought was a well-considered decision. In one of my first letters home, I told Mary that my plate was quite full with my role as a father and husband, my full-time work for the school district, my part-time work at a convenience store, and my graduate school studies (to become a school psychologist, a position that would increase my salary considerably). I realized that the additional time and stress of teaching that Sunday school class had been just too much for me; it was overwhelming. I wrote that when I returned I was going to carefully consider any new callings or positions that the local church leaders would ask of me (and that I was *not* going to return to teaching that particular youth group again). I stated that if any proposed church job or calling was going to significantly interfere with other important aspects of my life—especially my time and relationships with my family—I would turn down any such requests. I added that I would be willing to accept a Church calling if the time (and the stress associated with it) were *not* going to get in the way of my other responsibilities, but that I had to place my own health and sanity—and my family—first.

The reply I received from Mary surprised me, although I should have expected it. In her letter, Mary informed me that my proposal was in direct opposition to the teachings, customs, and directions of the church. She vehemently objected to my potential refusal of accepting a calling that she and the church leaders believed was being given to me directly by God.

Furthermore, this letter actually contained a threat of *divorce* if I continued to maintain this position. Mary truly put every aspect of the Mormon Church above me and our relationship. This turned out to be the first of many similar divorce threats I would receive from her over the next several years.

Another stressor in our family—which combined both financial and religious factors—was the issue of the payment of tithing (and other funds) to the LDS Church. Although they regularly ask for contributions to a number of different funds and projects (such as Missionary Fund, Ward Budget, Fast Offerings, Temple Building Funds, etc.), the Mormon Church instructs its members that they are *required* to pay 10 percent of their financial "increase" to the church (many church leaders interpret tithing as 10 percent of one's gross salary, before any deductions). In fact, for those members who have gone through the Mormon Church temple ceremony—which is highly encouraged for all adults—these members promise to give themselves, their time, their talents, and everything which they now have, or may have in the future, to the LDS church as part of that ceremony (in light of that, perhaps 10 percent is not too much to ask). In any event, this tithing requirement caused problems for me, and for us.

Lastly, I was constantly living on a financial precipice, and virtually everything I made was required to pay bills, provide a home, and to buy food. There really was no excess. For Mary, however, the church requirement to pay tithing superseded *everything* else. The Mormon Church actually teaches that their tithing requirement should be their members' highest priority, and it should be paid *prior* to any and all other household bills or expenses, regardless of the consequences to the member (including if payment of tithing to the church results in not having the funds necessary to pay rent, mortgage, utility bills, medical care, food, etc.). The church teaches that *it* is to be paid first.

After our children were born, there came a point when we could not pay a full tithe to the church. My solution was to cut back on contributions to the church so that I could continue to feed, clothe, and house our children. After a few years of not paying this tithe, Mary became quite uneasy and requested that we begin doing so, even when it was clear that we could not afford it. She put her faith in the unseen "blessings" that were promised, while I put my faith in mathematics and the numbers written on a sheet of paper showing our monthly budget.

This disagreement continued for quite some time until Mary decided to go back to work; she obtained a part-time job as teacher at a junior high school. However, the money that Mary earned did not go to help the family through food, clothing, transportation, or housing. She obtained her job and earned this money for the specific purpose of paying a full tithe to the Mormon Church. Mary's dedication to this principle was such that she paid tithing on *both* our salaries, not just hers alone. This took a majority of her salary to accomplish. But this was, after all, *her* salary, and if paying most of her money to the church was something that she wanted to do, that was fine with me. What I did not realize at the time, however, was that Mary silently resented this situation (that she was paying most of her salary to the church and *I* was not giving them anything from my own salary). As for myself, I was harboring resentment over the interference that the Mormon Church was having in our lives.

The future did not look bright for us...

Sixteen

Lisbeth

A daughter is a gift of love.
—Unknown

At the time that Lisbeth was born, she was the fourth child in my "second" family; at that time, Karl was six and a half years old, Marit was five, and Peder was two.

Lisbeth was born on the same calendar date of my mother's birthday. Because of that, I'm certain that my mother would have held a special place in her heart for Lisbeth, possibly even making Lisbeth one of her favorites (my mother was much kinder to her grandchildren than she was to her own children). Unfortunately, my mother had died after an extended bout with cancer three and half years before Lisbeth was born.

Shortly after Lisbeth's birth, we discovered that she had a skin condition that was similar to that of her older brother, Karl; they both had eczema. For Lisbeth, this condition included deep cracks in her skin. We treated her daily with various medications and creams (as directed by her doctor). Nevertheless, before she was one year old, Lisbeth had to be hospitalized for a few days because of a staph infection that had entered her system through these skin cracks. It was so difficult (and sad) to see our little baby on the hospital bed with an intravenous line connected to a vein in her head, giving her antibiotics.

While Lisbeth was still quite young, her mother would occasionally have trouble getting her to sleep at night. Often, Mary would become flustered and just bring Lisbeth into our bedroom and lay her next to me and leave. Lisbeth would then squirm and crawl over to me and put her head into the center of my back. She would then spend several minutes pressing the top of her head hard against me. This physical contact with me seemed to settle her somehow, and she would usually fall asleep after a few minutes. Later, when Mary went to bed, she would move a soundly sleeping Lisbeth back to her crib.

With all my children, I tried to find how I could make them laugh. Usually, I could tickle my babies through their stomachs, beginning when they were several weeks old. Lisbeth, however, didn't respond like the rest of the children—at first. When I initially tried to tickle Lisbeth, she didn't laugh. Instead, her stomach muscles tensed up and she grunted, and her grunt sounded sort of like a bear's growl. From that point on, Lisbeth's nickname was "Bear," and so she was variously called Liz, Lizzy, Liz-Bear, or just Bear by her immediate family.

Interestingly, Liz later became one of the most ticklish people I have ever seen. She was *extremely* ticklish, and she would even curl up in a ball and begin laughing if she even saw someone just approaching her with the intent of trying to tickle her.

I once conducted a little experiment with Liz when she was about twelve or thirteen years old. All of our family was in the living room one evening when I suggested this exercise. Liz agreed to be blindfolded, and the objective was to see if Liz could detect when someone's hand was near her body with the intent of tickling her. After several trials, I was quite impressed with the results. Liz was able to perceive when a hand was within about six inches from her body, and she responded with laughter as if she was actually being tickled. If the person's hand was farther away from her, there was no reaction. Lizzy was truly the most ticklish person I'd known—one didn't even need to *touch* to tickle her.

Liz was an above-average student at school and always did well (particularly at the lower grade levels). At one point—when she was in the second grade—I noticed that she was consistently getting perfect, 100 percent scores on her weekly spelling tests. This was great, but I also viewed this as an indication that perhaps Liz was not being challenged enough with her classwork. I approached Liz's classroom teacher (which was in one of the schools to which I was assigned to work as a school psychologist), and asked if it would be possible to give Lisbeth more difficult spelling tasks. This occurred in February, around Valentine's Day. As an example of more a challenging spelling assignment, I jokingly suggested that maybe Liz could learn to spell "I love you" in different languages, and I showed the teacher some examples. The following week, Liz came home with the results of her spelling test—she got another 100 percent! But this test was different: her teacher actually used the examples I had shared with her, and so Liz's personal test that week consisted of writing "I love you" in English, French, German, Norwegian, and Russian (using the Cyrillic Russian alphabet). Liz told me that she would rather work with the regular class spelling lists, and she asked me not to make any more suggestions to her teacher.

Over the years, Liz's eczema was difficult to control. She had to keep her skin—especially her hands—constantly moisturized, and she had to apply anti-itch medicine and cortisone creams. Still, this condition plagued her. One evening, when she was probably nine years old, one of her brothers brought her to me while I was sitting in the living room. He wanted me to see what Liz had done. Liz showed me her wrists, which were quite bloody from her scratching. I cleaned off her blood with a gauze pad moistened with rubbing alcohol. Of course, this stung so badly that she cried as I worked on her. Afterward, I bandaged her wrists. A few days later, however, Liz again scratched her wrists until they bled. That was the point when I realized how powerful the urge was to scratch—that her need to scratch herself was actually uncontrollable (since she would risk the pain of having her wounds cleaned again with such a stinging substance). Facing me that evening, there was a fear in her eyes that devastated me—she was afraid that I was going to hurt her again by using rubbing alcohol. Instead, I cleaned the blood off with water, dried her skin, and applied a first aid antibiotic ointment. I again applied new gauze pads and wrapped her wrists with gauze strips. The next day, I bought a full supply of gauze rolls, pads, ointment, and tape. I decided I would just keep cleaning and bandaging her wounds as long as necessary.

Besides her eczema, Liz occasionally had difficulty with asthma and bronchitis, and she had to use a nebulizer and inhalers to help clear her breathing passageways. This was difficult for her, because Liz was always so energetic. When she was young, Liz appeared to have two speeds: "fast" and "off." she maintained a high energy level when she was awake but would usually sleep soundly during the night.

But the more active she became, the more her breathing problems would interfere with her activity. Liz's respiratory problems did cause another hospitalization for her when she was in about the fourth grade. She had been sick for a few days with a fever, and our home remedies (nebulizer, over-the-counter medicines, etc.) didn't seem to work, so I took her to the doctor. After his examination, the doctor said that she had pneumonia and needed to be hospitalized for a few days so she could get the appropriate treatment.

Liz cried softly when she heard the doctor say that; she didn't want to go. But since she knew she had to go and that it was for her well-being, she went. Again, it was very difficult for me to leave my child in a hospital. I stayed with her for a long time when she was admitted, and I helped show her where everything was in her room and how it all worked. Liz's outlook on her situation visibly improved when I demonstrated the use of the remote control for the television set and the call button for the nurse's station. Over the next few days, Liz made liberal use of both of these controls.

As a school psychologist, my work schedule and duties at that time were somewhat flexible, so I was able to stop by the hospital at different times of the day as I traveled back and forth between school buildings. On one of my stops, I brought Liz a "Get Well" balloon bouquet attached to a small basket with a scraggly looking teddy bear inside. As I passed the stuffed bear to her through the oxygen tent that surrounded her, I was surprised at her reaction: Liz *loved* that shabby bear, and she immediately named it "Hospital" (since that was where she was when she received it). This became one of her most prized possessions.

When any of my children were ill and could not go to school, they stayed home alone (when they were old enough). I would call throughout the day to check on them. I also started a tradition of calling on these mornings and asking what they wanted for lunch that day. Then, I would pick up whatever food they chose and bring it to them. We then ate lunch together. Due to her frequent illnesses, it seemed that Liz was the recipient of this service more than the other children. Almost invariably, Liz would choose chicken strips for lunch (which I would dutifully bring to her). In fact, Liz became quite the connoisseur of this dish, ordering chicken strips almost every time we went to a restaurant or fast-food establishment to eat. Another of Liz's favorite foods was popsicles (in almost any flavor). If there were no popsicles left in the freezer, Liz was sure to let people know whenever they went shopping.

I used to receive periodic e-mail notifications from a few airline companies whenever they had special notices or sales that they wanted to publicize. At one point, I received an e-mail notification from one airline announcing the beginning of a new, direct flight from Minncapolis to Oslo, Norway. The offer was for a substantially reduced rate (I think it was about $399 for a round-trip ticket). That was a phenomenally low price. The catch was that the flight had to be booked within a few days of that e-mail, and the trip had to start the following week. Although I had tried to maintain current passports for all my children (one never knows when they might need it), only Lisbeth had a valid passport. It was the beginning of her fifth grade year. I decided to make this trip and take Lisbeth with me. She agreed to this trip, as did her mother. Unfortunately, there was not enough time to get our other children's passports renewed before the airline offer expired.

At that point, I remembered that my father (who still lived in Salt Lake City) also had a valid passport, since he had previously considered a trip back to the old country but had not done so (yet). I immediately called him and asked him if he would like to accompany us. I would have loved to have traveled with him and to have him show me places where he went and listened to stories of what he did as a child, as a teenager, and as an adult in Norway. This would have helped me connect more with him and our place of birth and to try to understand him better. Also, I was sure that both he and Lisbeth would have enjoyed this time together and get to know each other better.

When I telephoned my father I laid out all the factors: he was retired and had no time-pressing obligations, he had a passport, the airline flight was dirt cheap (with only one connection), I would be with him so he would have no problems navigating the airports, his brother in Norway had invited my father to stay with him, and our relatives in Norway were excited about the possibility of his visit (I had contacted several of them in Norway before calling my father). Several times over the previous years, I had asked my father to come with me on a trip to Norway, but he had always declined. But this time, everything seemed to fall into place, and I thought this was a great opportunity. Nevertheless, after hemming and hawing a bit, my father declined again, saying, "I don't feel very well." I was disappointed. He seemed fine to me, but I had no idea what hidden health problems he may have had at that time. Nevertheless, that was the last time I asked him.

Many years later, when my father was physically too frail to make such a trip, he made the comment to my sister that maybe he *should* have returned to Norway after his retirement. We all have life regrets.

So, it was just Liz and me on this trip. It would have been a better experience with my father along, but we were still going to have our own adventure. I applied for my personal leave from work, and we arranged for Liz to take a week off from school (taking with us her homework). The total trip took about nine days.

Lisbeth had quite an adventurous spirit for such a young girl and was very excited to go. When we boarded our first flight (Lisbeth's first time on a plane), she happened to turn to the left after she stepped onto the aircraft, rolling her little suitcase behind her. Of course, the stewardess blocked her way and told her she couldn't enter the cockpit (the door was open so that we could see the pilot and copilot in their seats). When Lisbeth was stopped by the flight attendant, however, she turned and stepped back *off* the plane. I was right behind her and stood in her way.

"It's OK, Liz," I said. "Even though they won't let you fly the plane, you can still get on." I then directed her to the right, toward the rows of seats.

Luckily, we had been upgraded to first class for that particular flight, so Lisbeth enjoyed the luxury of that service for her first experience in a plane. When I gave her a brief explanation of how things worked—including the flight attendant call button—Liz fit right in. She seemed to treat these controls just as she had when she was in the hospital; she knew what they were for and wasn't shy in using them when she needed to, but she also didn't misuse them.

Lisbeth and I enjoyed our whirlwind trip, and she loved the experience. We went to a few tourist spots and met several of my relatives (cousins and an uncle). Liz got to eat authentic Norwegian food. After the trip was over, she often told me that she wanted to return and to stay longer next time. I told her that we certainly could do that. From that point on, I sometimes called Lisbeth "my pretty little Viking girl." She liked that appellation.

As my children were growing up, we would usually make an annual trip to LaGoon, an amusement park in northern Utah. We enjoyed the special rides and activities during the day, and we stayed at a classy hotel during the evening. Lisbeth particularly enjoyed taking advantage of the hotel's room service (with permission, of course); she liked being catered to.

Lisbeth was smaller in stature than my other children. I've always wondered if this was at least partly because of the medical problems she had as well as the treatments and medications that she was taking. But she was still very active and very adventurous.

When she was in junior high school, Liz was active in her school's track program (the hurdles). She also wanted to play soccer, but Mary didn't let her; she said that Liz was too small for that sport. When Marit went rock climbing one weekend with her boyfriend, Liz happily joined them. I didn't go with them at that time, but I did see photographs from that expedition. Liz looked happy and quite at ease, hanging by ropes on the rock cliff with her helmet and protective gear on.

As Liz grew older, she took on more and more responsibilities, and she enjoyed the additional obligations that came with them. She babysat often, and really enjoyed children. She worked with them well, and they responded to Liz's personality. Liz would comment that one of her life goals was to marry and have a family with her own children in the future.

Liz was also planning on going to college, and—like her brothers and sister—had a bank account dedicated to that goal (to which I contributed a small amount monthly). Whenever Liz earned some money herself, or had received some money as a gift, I took her to the bank to encourage her to put some of this money into her college fund. Liz resisted this idea and wanted to immediately spend it all on things and activities so she could enjoy them *now*. It would take some talking to convince her, but she would usually agree to put part of this money away for her future. I was trying to get her into the habit of saving something now so that she could have money available to meet her expenses at college. From my own personal experience, I knew how important that was.

When she was fifteen-and-a-half years old, Liz was also proud of the fact that she had passed the written examination for her driver's license on her first attempt (her older brother had apparently failed the first time *he* took this test). She was looking forward to taking the actual driving lessons, passing the practical exam, and receiving her license. This meant more freedoms and responsibilities, and it also meant that she was growing up.

On another occasion (at about this same time), I had taken Lisbeth to the airport, as she was booked to take a direct flight to her destination (about a one-and-a-half-hour flight). This was to be her first experience flying alone. When we got to the airport, we found that her flight was delayed for about two hours. There really wasn't time to go home and return again, so I decided to wait there. After sitting for a while, occasionally talking but spending most of the time watching people come and go, Lisbeth then suggested that I could leave her there. She said that she knew how to find the gate and board the plane on her own. She said she'd done it several times before; she knew how it all worked. I said that I wanted to stay with her, and I told her that whenever I had taken my children to the airport before with her brothers, I always stayed until their plane was boarded, it taxied from the gate, and its wheels actually lifted off the ground. Only then would I leave.

"But I'm a big girl," she said. "You don't have to babysit me."

"But I *want* to be here with you," I replied. "Besides, there might be a problem and the plane gets delayed again."

"I'll be OK," Liz insisted. "I can handle it."

I knew that she was capable. I didn't like the thought of my little girl growing up and becoming independent, although I knew it was inevitable. I decided to try a new tack.

"Well, they might announce a new delay for the plane," I started.

"I can handle it," she repeated.

"And then maybe another delay. What if they cancel the flight altogether? Then what will you do?"

"I'll get a motel room. There are hotels right next to the airport."

"Yes, and do you have the money to pay for it?" I said, starting to lay it on thick. "Sometimes, the airlines will give food and hotel vouchers if they cancel a flight. Do you know how these work? How will you wake up in the morning? Do you have an alarm clock? If you don't get vouchers, do you have money enough for dinner, the hotel, and breakfast tomorrow?"

After a pause, Liz said dejectedly, "OK. I guess you can stay."

I was happy—I enjoyed spending every minute I could with her. But I knew Lisbeth was becoming a young adult and would soon be meeting the challenges of life on her own, but I also knew I would miss my little girl who depended on me.

Even though Liz was growing up and maturing, she still occasionally did things that were immature. These events were sometimes humorous as well. That same morning that I took Liz to the airport, she needed to clean her room because it was a complete mess; the floor was literally covered with clothes, stuffed animals, games, books, and other belongings. Liz sat in the middle of all this, intently playing a game of SIMS on the computer.

When I asked her to clean her room, Liz answered, "OK, Pappa," without looking up from the computer screen.

After about half an hour, I walked by her room again. Liz was still playing and hadn't moved from her chair (that game was so addicting to her).

"Liz," I said, "you've *got* to get this room cleaned before we go."

"Yeah, I know."

"Well?"

"OK, OK!"

A few minutes later, I saw that Liz had *still* not budged from her chair in front of the computer.

"Liz!" I said. "If this room is not cleaned within the next fifteen minutes, you're not going!"

Liz got to work. Fifteen minutes later, I was surprised to see that the room *was* clean, except for a couple of items still left on the floor. I was amazed, and I complimented her. "Great job!"

After I returned from the airport that afternoon, I went into her room and picked up the two remaining items that were left on the floor, and I opened the closet door to see where I could put them. That's when I saw how Liz was able to clean the room so quickly. As I pulled open the folding doors to the closet, I was greeted with a stack of clothes, books, stuffed animals—*everything*—all haphazardly stacked and crammed into a solid pile in the closet to height of about five feet. Liz had apparently opened the closet doors, thrown everything in there, balanced it all so that it would not fall down, and shut the doors again.

Lisbeth found a way to bend my rules; she *did* clean up her room as I asked, but not in the way I expected.

Clever girl.

Seventeen

The Second Divorce

When people divorce, it's always such a tragedy.
At the same time, if people stay together it can be even worse.
—*Monica Bellucci*

L ooking back, I can see that—at that point—I finally had
accomplished several things that I wanted (or needed) in
my life. I had a family, and I was a father again. Although I
still remembered and missed Erik every day, I had five living
children whom I loved deeply and tried to keep happy and
healthy. If these were *all* the factors that were involved in my
life, I would've thought that life was good—*very* good.

But of course, life is not that simple.

Besides the normal stressors that most people experience
(who are trying to raise five children), I had the additional
anxieties of living with my low self-esteem, worrying about the
stability of my employment, and my graduate study course-
work. On top of these, I was dealing with the differences Mary
and I had regarding the role of the LDS Church in our lives,
particularly about tithing (it became quite clear that our pri-
orities differed greatly).

It was at about this time that I began to be more critical of the way things operated in the Mormon Church, as well as with some of their specific beliefs and practices. Some of my criticisms involved generally accepted Christian beliefs, including literal belief of the stories of Noah and the flood, Moses receiving stone tablets inscribed by God and his parting of the Red Sea, Job being tortured and punished as the object of a wager between God and Satan, and Jonah living inside of a whale. Like many Christian churches, the Mormon Church taught these stories as literal truths. I couldn't buy it.

One Bible story that caused me particular angst was the one about Abraham almost sacrificing and killing his own son just to please God. As a father who had actually lost a child to death, I could not understand how *any* father would even *consider* doing such a thing to his own child, no matter *who* told him to do it. One Sunday, during a priesthood class at church, this story was related by the teacher and held up as an example of how we should be willing to obey God's commandments, no matter how we feel about it at the time. Being very tired of having held my opinions to myself for many years, I finally spoke up. I pointed out that if one actually looks carefully at what Abraham was doing, it was *not* a good thing; it was *not* an example to follow. I asked those in the class to look at this incident from Isaac's viewpoint.

"How do you think Isaac felt," I began, "having his father—the one man he should trust more than anyone in the world—grabbing him, tying him up, placing him on an altar, and then getting ready to cut his throat? That was a *horrible* thing to do and would have terrified Isaac." After a pause, I continued. "If this same thing happened in this country today, in *these* times the father would be arrested for attempted murder, or at least child endangerment, and rightly so. I think that, when someone—*anyone*—tells us to do something, we need to look at it first and decide for ourselves whether or not it is the right thing to do." I was not trying to be funny; I was quite sincere in my remarks.

After I had my say, there were no comments or reply from the class instructor or the other class participants—only silence. They then closed the meeting, since the time allotted for the class was nearly up. This was one example of an important principle in the Mormon Church: conformance and obedience are highly valued and individual thought is discouraged. It is a very common practice to *not* ask questions or to have meaningful discussions of lesson topics during classes or meetings. This is borne out by the following 1945 Mormon Church statement (and has been repeated in various forums over the years): "When our leaders speak, the thinking has been done." If a member has a different opinion than that which is in the official lesson manual, you are to either change your opinion to conform, or you are to keep quiet. I cannot keep quiet when I disagree with fundamental positions of an organization I belong to, and I do not understand how others *can* remain still.

I also had problems understanding what I considered to be many instances of dishonesty coming from church leaders, both at the local and at the highest levels, especially when truthfulness and honesty are constantly preached in church. I'll cite a few examples. In a 1997 *Time* magazine article interview, Gordon B. Hinckley (who was then president of the Mormon Church as well as claiming to be a living prophet of God) was asked, "Is this the teaching of the church today, that God the Father was once a man like we are?"

Hinkley replied, "I don't know that we teach it. I don't know that we emphasize it. I haven't heard it discussed for a long time in public discourse. I don't know."

I was astounded at this response. This "God was once a man" concept is a basic, core principle of Mormon Church doctrine. When I read this, I pulled out my current LDS priesthood manual and saw that this belief was the subject of one of that year's lessons. And Hinkley—the highest *leader* of the Church—*denied* it!

Another example of dishonesty (at the local level) occurred when we—as a congregation—were introduced to a young father who had just been baptized and had joined the church. In the priesthood meeting that Sunday morning, this man had also been ordained to the Aaronic priesthood. Later that day, during Sacrament meeting, this father's newborn baby was being blessed. For this ordinance, several men stand in a circle with one man holding the baby and each of the others having one hand under the child. Then, one man gives a prayer and bestows a blessing on the child. Normally, these men are those who have the Melchizedek priesthood (the next step up from the basic Aaronic priesthood). However, in the priesthood manual, it stated that if the father of the child had only the Aaronic priesthood, he could still be included in this circle and thus participate in the blessing of his own child (even though he cannot give the actual blessing, since that required someone with Melchizedek priesthood authority). I saw that this young father was excluded from this blessing circle. After the services were over, I asked one of the bishopric counselors why this young father was not allowed to participate. "I'm sure he really would've loved to have been included," I said.

"Because he doesn't hold the Melchizedek priesthood," was the reply. "Only those with the Melchizedek priesthood can be in the circle."

"But there's an exception for the father," I said, and I showed him the information I had found in my current priesthood manual.

After looking at the passage, the counselor said dismissively, "Well, we received a letter last month from Salt Lake changing that." He then turned and walked away.

I knew he was lying; by his demeanor I knew there was no such letter. The bishop's counselor just said that to cover himself and not have to admit that they perhaps had made a mistake and didn't realize that the father was allowed to be in the circle. It may have been a "little" lie to him, but it bothered me that these church leaders found it so easy to be dishonest regarding Church doctrines, teachings, policies, and procedures. They unnecessarily denied the father of this baby from participating in a special ordinance for this child, and then refused to acknowledge that they might have made a mistake in this decision.

This attitude of mine led to more problems with Mary. As I was experiencing more difficulties with some of the doctrines, policies, and practices associated the Mormon Church, I began to share these concerns and opinions with her. That was a mistake. Instead of discussing these issues and concerns with me or even expressing her own viewpoint, she either dismissed my opinions outright or remained silent. But apparently—just below the surface—she was seething with anger and resentment. I believe that the root of this anger stems from another proscription from the church: Thou shalt not criticize or speak ill about the church or it leaders in any way, whatsoever. This prohibition has often been voiced by the church leaders at all levels. Dallin Oakes, one of the current Mormon Church apostles, stated in a PBS documentary, "It's wrong to criticize leaders of the church, even if the criticism is true." I didn't follow that advice.

The gist of all this was that Mary and I were both changing. I had thought we were on the same track when we first married, but now I was drifting further and further away from the Mormon Church while Mary appeared to be getting ever *closer* to the church. We were now on different trains, headed in opposite directions. Unfortunately for me, Mary's destination was to join with those who positioned the Mormon Church as the highest priority in their lives.

After I first received my first divorce threat from Mary (that summer when I was attending school in Olso), I continued to receive a number of similar threats from her over the following years. During this period, Mary also moved out of our bedroom and slept in a makeshift room that she had set up in our basement.

Our relationship continued to sour as time progressed. At one point, however, I decided to make a couple of conciliatory gestures.

In one instance, I ordered a bouquet of flowers for Mary and had them delivered anonymously to our house. I had the florist sign it, "From a Secret Admirer." I was home when they were delivered, and I saw Mary's face light up when she received them. She was very excited. But then, Mary's next step baffled me; she started wondering *who* could have sent them. First, she called her Visiting Teachers from the church. No, she was told, they hadn't sent them. Then she called her parents and her siblings. They hadn't sent them either. Then she started calling all of the friends and acquaintances that she could think of, and she never could identify her secret admirer. After several hours of this, I finally told Mary that *I* had sent them (I was wondering who she was thinking of calling next). Her response was,

"Oh. I thought I had asked you" (she had not). This event told me a lot about the status of our relationship in her mind; she didn't even consider that I might have been an admirer.

On another occasion, I asked Mary if she'd like to go for some long walks with me, perhaps two or three times a week. I wanted to schedule these in order to give us some alone time together when we could talk, and I figured it was also a good way to get some exercise. She used to go out jogging before (and shortly after) we were married, and she only stopped when she started having babies. However, Mary didn't even think about doing this with me—she immediately declined my suggestion.

"My joints ache," she said. "I'm getting older, and my hips hurt when I walk too much."

I was somewhat surprised when—several months after telling me that she was getting too old and frail to go for walks with me—I saw Mary out going on a very brisk walk with one of her assigned Visiting Teaching project women, and they were sharing these exercise events on a regular basis. I thought that Mary might be doing this for one of two possible reasons: either she was putting up with painful hip joints in order to help fulfill this church calling or she was just making up excuses to avoid going with *me* when I asked that we take walks together. Either way, I saw that I was not very important to her and that others always came first.

Shortly following these incidents—and after our "in-house separation" had gone on for three years—I finally tired of Mary's continuing divorce threats and accepted the next one that came my way.

"Yes, I think we *do* need to divorce," I said in the end.

Thus began the formal dissolution of my second marriage and my second family, and it was another example of my self-identity as a failure at life.

Once this decision had been made, I noted that Mary seemed almost giddy with excitement. No longer was she the good *listener* (the person to whom others came for a sympathetic ear). Now *Mary* was the one with a sad tale of woe— now *she* was one who needed sympathy and comforting. She appeared to quite enjoy this role reversal.

Mary immediately went to our local Mormon Church leaders, the bishopric. After returning from one of these meetings with the bishop, I asked her what had transpired. I was curious to see what the church would do in our situation, since they were constantly presenting themselves as being supporters of the family and claimed to value committed family relationships. I wanted to see if they would also *act* on these proclamations and do something to try to hold our family together.

"He asked if there was anything he could do for us," Mary said.

"What did you say to that?"

"I asked him if he knew of any rental places you could move into," she replied. "And here's a list of places he gave me." She handed me a slip of paper with the names of four local landlords and their telephone numbers.

I remember thinking, *So that's how they support and strengthen families. Not a word about trying to find out what's wrong and what can be done to fix the marriage, just a list of landlords so she can get me out of the house ASAP.*

I soon discovered that Mary was receiving free legal advice from a former Mormon Church bishop (who was a lawyer). During the following few weeks, I noticed that *nobody* from the church tried to contact me to find out what was happening or to see if they could help us stay together in any way. Our Home Teachers stopped coming over, my elder's quorum presidency didn't say a word, none of the bishopric talked to me (although they seemed quite willing to talk with Mary), and those whom I had thought were my friends never said a word.

I really viewed this as a life lesson. This organization that proclaimed itself to be supportive of families through its scriptures, general conference speeches, teachings, and lessons in priesthood meetings, Relief Society and Sunday school (and that spent a *lot* of money on advertising these professed values to the public), did *nothing* to help keep our family together. They didn't even *offer*.

I once mentioned this fact to Mary. I pointed out how she was being assisted by everyone we knew to help *end* our marriage, while no one offered to help us keep it *together* (in fact, no one from the church even spoke to me at all about this during this ordeal). I asked her why I was being ignored. She thought for a moment and replied, "Maybe it's because they think I'm a better Mormon than you." I really think she was right.

It took a few months, but the deed was finally done. We were divorced. Mary and the children remained in our old house; Mary didn't even want them to stay overnight with me in my new apartment. ("They need to sleep in their own beds every night.") I could see them when there wasn't anything else going on (such as meetings or activities)—otherwise, overnight visits with me would "upset their schedules."

This arrangement continued for three years, until our two oldest children had graduated from high school. After that, Mary took our three youngest children with her to live in her parents' house in Oregon. Karl and Marit remained in Idaho.

Mary got a teaching job in Oregon, and she said that her salary and benefits were so much better there than they had been in our local school district in Idaho. We agreed that she would cover our children on her medical insurance policy ("family" medical coverage was part of her benefit package) while I would pay for transporting them back and forth between Portland and Boise for their visits. Mary also announced that two of her brothers (who both lived within a hundred yards of their parents' home) would serve as *my* children's father figures. In her eyes, I was so easily replaceable.

After their move, I flew the children to and from Idaho during school breaks and long weekends. With this arrangement, however, I finally got to actually live *with* my children again (at least for these short periods); I could again tuck them in bed at night, make them breakfast and other meals, take them places, or just *be* with them. Of course, it was almost unbearably lonely when my children were gone, but when they were with me, life was better—it felt almost normal.

There is one constant in life, and that is that things *always* change. Our visitation arrangement concerning our children changed again when Mary found a new beau…

Eighteen

Lightning Strikes Again

Lightning is something which, again, we would rather avoid.
—*Richard Branson*

My three youngest children remained in Oregon for three years. They apparently took turns living in Mary's parents' house, or in a garage directly behind their house that was being divided into bedrooms and outfitted with a small bathroom (toilet and sink). I disliked the constant, extremely close proximity that my children had with their grandparents, but there was nothing I could do about this. These grandparents acted like they were my children's parents and kept telling them that I was a bad influence and that they should stay away from me. Mary seemed to prefer this living arrangement, as she never did find a separate place (an apartment or a house) where she and the children could live independently during the entire time they stayed in Oregon.

One of the few things that Mary told me about her own childhood was the fact that her father would occasionally threaten to beat her and her siblings with a belt for various behavioral infractions. She added that he did follow through with these threats if the children did not obey. Mary said that she had been whipped with her father's belt when she and her siblings failed to go to their beds at the appointed hour or when—after getting in their beds—they continued talking to each other rather than going to sleep.

This, I thought, was insane.

Occasionally, when talking with my children, I asked them about the types of discipline that they were experiencing. They commented that their mother would automatically assume that her own children were at fault whenever there was any dispute or complaint from other children or their parents ("she never sticks up for us" was a common complaint). At one point, however, I was told that Mary's father had actually pulled out his belt from his pants and threatened to whip my two younger children with it (the older son was then in high school and would have been able to defend himself quite effectively). Mary's father did not threaten to hurt those who could fight back. Mary was apparently not at home when this first occurred. My children said that their grandfather did not actually strike them yet, but he did threaten to do so (and they were concerned that he would).

Knowing that such threats—unless checked—often escalate to eventual action, I told my children that they did not have to accept such behaviors, and I instructed them to call the police if it ever actually occurred or if they were afraid that it would happen. I told them to dial 911 because such an event *would* be an emergency. When I next spoke with Mary, I told her what was happening between her father and the children, and I told her what I had instructed the children to do.

Mary's reaction was somewhat surprising to me, but I probably should have expected it. She turned to the children and said, "You can't call the police on your grandfather!" No thought about protecting the children—just protecting her father.

These three younger children were scheduled to be with me for at least six weeks each summer. All went well that first summer, but when the second summer came, only two of my children arrived. The older boy, Peder, stayed in Oregon. I was told that he needed to remain there because he was looking for work. Someone apparently decided that his prospects for finding summer or part-time employment in Oregon were better than his prospects would be in Idaho (where he would only be available for the summer). At least that is what they told me.

I wasn't too happy about the fact that Peder's *possible* employment in Oregon was more important than visiting or being with me, but he was getting older and needed this important life experience, his first job. I acquiesced, even though I wasn't sure I actually had any real choice in the matter. As it turned out, Peder never did find a job in Oregon, neither that summer nor during the following school year. This meant that I lost out on having one more summer with him and spending that allotted time with him.

As the third summer of their experience in Oregon approached, Mary's life was changing; she had connected with a man named Dan, who appeared to be everything she wanted: a staunch member of the Mormon Church. As summer approached, Mary and Dan made plans to be married.

The problem for Mary was that Dan lived in Idaho and didn't want to leave, so she decided to move back. Mary ended up purchasing a house that was approximately fifteen miles from where I was living and about ten miles in the other direction from where Dan lived. Mary spent much of that summer making preparations for her move.

As this summer approached, I was informed that Lisbeth had failed some of her ninth grade courses during the previous school year. As a result, Mary told me that Lisbeth should stay in Oregon that summer so she could retake these classes before transferring schools. I protested; I explained that my local high school also offered summer courses, and Lisbeth could easily take them while living with me (which was, by the way, where she was *supposed* to be that summer). Mary, however, said that it was important that the makeup courses be the same as those she'd failed, and my local school might not have the exact classes she needed. Lisbeth stayed in Oregon that third summer.

One of the reasons why I acquiesced to permitting Lisbeth to stay in Oregon for that summer was because Liz was seriously considering living with me for the following school year (her tenth grade year). In previous years, after my breakup with Mary, Lisbeth had occasionally expressed a desire to live with me (rather than with her mother) for at least one year. Whenever Lisbeth expressed this wish to her mother, Mary had refused, explaining, "You need me, and I need you." Again, *I* was superfluous and unimportant—this statement implied that my children didn't *really* need me, and I didn't *really* need my children. Not true at all.

But now Lisbeth was getting older and was able to have a greater voice in who she wanted to live with, and she eventually decided that she wanted to live with me. Once I knew that that was her wish, I was prepared to go to court to reopen the custody agreement to make that happen (if that became necessary). As the summer progressed, it was becoming clear that Lisbeth was going to be with me that next school year.

One of the reasons that Lisbeth gave as to why she wanted to live with me was "because you'll make me do my homework."

Lisbeth recognized that she was capable of doing well at school but she was lacking structure, encouragement, and motivation.

As it turned out, Lisbeth did not pass any of her summer makeup classes, so that the extra time spent in Oregon was a total waste as well. She could easily have been with me that summer, as scheduled, and she could also have completed at least some of her needed courses.

Another problem with the scheduled visitation with my children that third summer was that Peder was again not staying with me. Peder was desperate to find summer work (after failing to find work in Oregon that entire previous year), and so Dan arranged to have Peder work at the same company where he was employed. Since both Peder and Dan would then be working at the same location, it was decided that it would be more convenient to have Peder stay and live with Dan that summer instead of with me. That way, they could travel to work and back together (their work location was approximately thirty miles from my house). Again, I was being pushed out, pushed aside. I was still unnecessary.

So, of the three children who were supposed to live at my house that summer, only my youngest son was with me.

As the summer was coming to an end, Lisbeth called me and asked if it would be all right if she could delay moving into my house for a week. She said she had an opportunity to stay with her oldest brother for that week (he was living temporarily in eastern Idaho at that time). Lisbeth and Karl were close, and she missed him very much during the previous two years that he served as a volunteer Mormon missionary in California. During such missions, the Church severely restricts contact between these missionaries and their families, limiting them to three telephone calls per year (Christmas, Mother's Day, and Father's Day). Other than that, the only communication that is allowed between these proselytizing missionaries and their family and friends is by written letters. These two years of severely limited contact was difficult for everybody, especially Lisbeth.

After Karl had returned from his mission, Lisbeth had only seen him for a couple of days, and she wanted to spend more time with him before school started. Even though I missed Lisbeth myself, I understood her desire and need to connect with Karl again. I agreed to this delay; I wasn't greedy. After all, Liz was shortly going to move into my house, and I was going to get to be her full-time father again, cooking her meals, giving her driving lessons, helping with her homework, being her advocate, and supporting her as she found her way through the maze of life during these teenage years. Liz and Karl needed each other at that point in time. I could wait.

As that week came to a close, I received another telephone call from Mary.

"We're taking the kids camping," she said.

"Who's *we?*" I asked.

"Dan and I," replied Mary. "We're taking the kids camping in Yellowstone for a week. I've got Peder and Gunnar Roy with me now, and we're going to pick up Lisbeth on the way."

"But Liz is supposed to be coming here," I protested. "That was the agreement I made with her when she went to Karl's. She stays with him for a week, and then she comes here."

"I've hardly seen Liz all summer," Mary argued. "And I need to spend time with her before school starts."

"What do you mean you haven't seen her all summer?" I asked, quite surprised. "She stayed in Oregon all summer. Where were you?"

"I was going back and forth to Idaho," she said, "getting ready for my move with interviews and house hunting. I really haven't been home much."

A horrible thought entered my mind: *Oh my God! Lisbeth was left alone with her grandparents all summer!* I later found out that Liz *had* suffered at the hands of her grandmother during that period. That woman had locked Lisbeth in her bedroom and refused to let her out or to let her have any food until she cleaned her room. Lisbeth can be quite stubborn, and my determined little girl ended up staying alone in that room nearly the entire day.

"It's not my fault you weren't in Oregon all summer," I retorted. "Liz is supposed to come here after she stayed with Karl this week. That was the deal."

"We're taking her camping," Mary said, concluding the debate. "She'll be back next week."

I felt frustrated. What could I do? Should I jump in my car and race across the state, trying to get ahead of Mary and Dan? Then, do I physically take Lisbeth from Karl's apartment and bring her back with me? I decided that there wasn't much I *could* do. I just had to wait another week, and then Liz would be with me. I try to be patient when I need to be, but patience has its limits.

Camping. That was something new for Mary. She had never been keen to go camping when we were married, but she seemed to be very interested in it now.

During one of their summers in Oregon, Mary had gone on a hiking and camping trip with our three youngest children.

Along on this trip was Mary's sister, Louise, and two of Louise's children. Their plan was to hike into the mountains, camp for the night, and then return the next day. What had actually happened, however, was a very different story (the details of which I learned much later).

Shortly after beginning on their hike, Louise had determined that her backpack was too heavy, and so she decided to lighten her load. Unfortunately, Louise was carrying much of the group's food, and she removed many of these items from her pack. I don't know if Louise first tried to redistribute these items to the other participants' backpacks (and perhaps they refused), but she ended up discarding this food at the side of the trail. With a lighter load to carry, Louise continued on the hike.

Eventually, however, the group discovered that they had ventured off the trail, and after fruitless efforts to find their bearings, it soon became evident that they were lost (and they had failed to bring any maps with them). At nightfall, the group made camp and ate what food they had. More efforts were made the following day to try to find either a trail or a logging road to follow (or even to meet some other hikers), but they were unable to do so.

What began as an overnight camp ended up being a lost journey lasting multiple days and nights. Of course, one major problem that soon arose was their lack of food. They attempted to ration what they had left, and at one point they had even made a "soup" that consisted of melting a cube of margarine in a pot of boiling water and drinking that. They soon became quite hungry.

After a few days, one of Louise's children (a teenage boy named Robert) became certain that he knew the way out and communicated this to the two adults of the group. Louise and Mary apparently didn't believe or share Robert's opinion and therefore did not follow his advice. The next day, a frustrated Robert left the group without permission and struck out on his own to find civilization.

It turned out that Robert *did* know what he was talking about and *was* able to contact the authorities. The following day, various search and rescue units combed the area, and a helicopter located the wayward hikers. A ground search team met them, gave them food, and led them out of the mountains.

I had not known about this camping trip beforehand and only learned about it after they had returned to their home. I had been trying to call my children for several days, and I was wondering why I could never get an answer.

As it turned out, my children were generally all right. Lisbeth, however, looked like what could best be described as a "baked potato." Her skin was brown from the overexposure to the sun, with prominent cracks visible all over (due to her eczema condition and not having enough moisturizing cream with her that she needed to apply daily). My precious little girl recovered after a few weeks.

Now, Mary and the kids were going camping again, this time with Dan. I did not know anything about Dan, so I didn't know if he had any familiarity with camping. But it was my understanding that this trip was *not* going to involve hiking into the mountains, but rather they were planning to use established campgrounds. That was better. I also hoped that Mary had learned from her earlier experience and that proper precautions would be taken.

Late that evening, I received a telephone call from Mary. She said that they had stopped at a campground in Yellowstone

Park and then went to go swimming in a nearby river. She told me that when the kids were swimming, Lisbeth drowned.

"What?"

"Lisbeth drowned. She's dead."

It took a moment for this information to sink in. Then, I screamed ... and *screamed!*

Nineteen

What Happened

Ever has it been that love knows not its own
depth until the hour of separation.
—*Khalil Gibran*

Something had gone terribly wrong on that camping trip.
When our children were small, we purchased a small, four-person, air-filled rubber raft to use during some of our weekend or summer outings. I had thought about using this raft to either just paddle around or to go fishing on one of the reservoirs not far from where we lived. Along with this raft, we also purchased four life vests: two adult sized and two child sized. There was no way that any of our children were going to go out on open water in that raft without safety gear. As it happened, we only used that raft once, taking turns rowing the children out onto the water. When we divorced, these life vests went with Mary and the children.

During the weeks following this latest tragedy, I tried to piece together what had happened that afternoon.

Mary, Dan, and my children had gone to a section of river in Yellowstone National Park called Firehole Canyon. It's my understanding that this was not an officially designated swimming area, but many people apparently used it as such. There is a section of this river where people jump in and are then carried by water current dozens of yards around a bend, where the swimmers are then deposited in a deeper, wide pool. Apparently, when they began this trip, the plan was that our children were also going to swim in this river, because they had brought and changed into their swimwear upon their arrival in the park.

First, Peder and Gunnar Roy went in for a few cycles of jumping in the river, being pulled by the current, and then being deposited into the pool. Lisbeth was sitting on the bank with Mary and Dan, watching them. Peder and Gunnar Roy called for Lisbeth to join them, telling her how fun it was. Lisbeth didn't want to go in at first, telling her mother that she didn't want to get her hair wet. Mary said that she repeatedly told Lisbeth, "It's your choice," as to whether or not to join her brothers. Ultimately, Lisbeth decided to join them in their fun.

I was told that Lisbeth jumped with her brothers into the river at the designated spot, and she followed them with the current. As they reached the deeper pool area, Lisbeth was holding Gunnar Roy's hand. Then—either because the river current still had hold of Lisbeth or perhaps her feet were caught in some vegetation or debris—she was being pulled under the water. The power of this drag proved to be too strong, and she was wrenched from her brother's hand, her head disappearing under the water. When he saw Lisbeth go under, Gunnar Roy said that he shouted for help.

When Lisbeth didn't resurface, all the other children apparently got out of the water, and the adults searched for Lisbeth. Some followed the riverbank downstream while others searched the pool. After about twenty minutes, Lisbeth was finally found not far from where she disappeared—her body was tangled among some weeds under a ledge with just her legs sticking out. After she was pulled from the river, CPR was administered by bystanders. Mary told me that *this* was the point in time at which emergency services were called. Upon their arrival, the paramedics continued with other efforts to try to revive her, but after an hour they decided it was too late. Lisbeth was dead.

The day after this incident, Yellowstone Park officials issued a press release describing what had happened to Lisbeth. At the end of the press release, they stated, "She was not wearing a life preserver, as the National Park Service strongly recommends."

Our children's life vests were sitting on a shelf in the garage of Mary's new house.

Lisbeth's death was an accident, but it was most certainly preventable.

Twenty

Another Funeral

*Death leaves a heartache no one can heal, love
leaves a memory no one can steal.*
—*Unknown*

When I was told that Lisbeth had died, I screamed. I was angry and upset, sad and depressed. A million emotions ran through my mind; I didn't know what to do.

I screamed so loud and so long that my voice was hoarse for nearly a week.

I called my oldest son, Karl. Lisbeth was staying with him when Mary picked her up to go camping. Oh, how I wished that she hadn't gone; I wished that I had said no more emphatically when Mary said Lisbeth was going with her. But they would've taken her anyway.

Karl said he didn't know anything about what had happened—no one had called him yet. He told me he'd try to find out.

I also telephoned Marit. She was living at a US Marine Corps base in North Carolina, going through a training program. At first, Marit didn't believe me, but she then said she'd try to come to Idaho as soon as she could when she understood that it was all too real.

I didn't know what else I could do. I was alone in my house. I didn't know who I could talk to or where I could go. I had lived in that house and had been working in that school district for one year, and I suddenly realized that I didn't have anyone in that area I could really call a friend, someone I could turn to in such an emergency. I was acquainted with many people who I worked with, of course, but they were coworkers, not close friends.

About forty minutes from the time I first received the dreadful news, my doorbell rang. It was a policeman. He said that they had received a call from someone (I learned later that it was Mary) who had asked them to check up on me. I let him in. I was surprised that she had done that.

I was upset and sobbing, but I managed to tell the officer what had happened. He seemed very concerned and asked if he could help in any way. I sensed that this man genuinely cared about me.

At that point, I remembered that I had a gun there in the house—a .22 caliber bolt-action rifle. I had owned this gun since I was a young teenager, and I had later used it to teach my children how to shoot. I had no plans at that time on using that gun—I wasn't feeling suicidal at that particular moment—but I didn't want the gun there at all, just in case. I asked if there was any way that he could take that rifle away and hold it for me, and he readily agreed. I retrieved the gun from my closet, and the officer pulled out a form and started filling it out (I remember being surprised at this, that there was actually a special form for police to use to receive and temporarily store weapons from civilians).

After placing the rifle in the trunk of his squad car, I asked the officer if he could take me to the local hospital. I had decided that I could not be alone (even without the gun), and I wanted to try to get checked into a hospital. I needed a sedative, and I needed to *not* be alone. The policeman readily agreed and drove me there. On the way, I remember being surprised at myself for the fact that—after living in that small community for a year—I didn't even know *where* the hospital was located. I lived on the southern edge of town, and I worked in the neighboring community that was south of where I lived, but still, I really *should've* known where the hospital was! That's how cloistered I was at that time; I went to work and to stores, but I generally stayed home instead of exploring and discovering my larger community.

When I arrived at the hospital, I talked to the employees in the emergency room and explained my situation. I got the impression that they were confused as to why I was there. I was not injured or hurt; there was nothing they could sew up or put a bandage on. I explained that I could *not* be alone that night. After a long wait and the same conversation with several other staff members, I was admitted as a psychiatric patient that night and given a sedative and a bed. I did manage to get some sleep, and I drew some comfort knowing that there were people nearby who were health professionals.

The following morning, I met with a psychiatrist who conducted a brief evaluation. By that time, I had calmed down somewhat. He released me to go home. I don't remember *how* I got home; I assume it was by taxi. It was such a confusing time.

My two youngest boys, Peder and Gunnar Roy, came to my house that next evening. It was good to see them, of course, but we were all upset over what had happened. Karl was coming to Boise himself, and Marit was on her way as well. She had received permission from her commander and made arrangements through the Red Cross to fly home.

My sons brought over some of Lisbeth's diaries to share with me. I didn't have time to read them all, but I scanned through them. It was comforting to be able to connect with her in this small way. In one entry, I noticed that Lisbeth wrote something about Erik. She wrote, "Pappa had a little boy before we were born. His name was Erik. He died in a car wreck. That must have been really sad for him."

That entry ripped my heart apart. I wanted to respond to my precious daughter: "Yes, Liz-Bear, that *was* sad. And I'm so very sad that you've died, too. My heart now breaks for both of you."

A short time later, I found that someone had removed these journals from my house and gave them to Mary. I felt that another part of Lisbeth was being taken away: her memories and thoughts. I wish I could've at least made copies of these diaries first.

The following day, I received a phone call from Mary in which she gave me details about Lisbeth's funeral arrangements. She said that if I wanted to have any input into this process, I would need to be at the funeral home the following morning. I went.

Mary had chosen the funeral home and the cemetery. I still owned the grave plot next to Erik (in Salt Lake City), and I offered to have Liz buried there. That offer was refused; I was told that Lisbeth would be buried in a cemetery in Boise.

Mary had also made arrangements to have the funeral service held in a local Mormon Church building. I *was* offered the opportunity to speak at the funeral, which I accepted.

Since the funeral service was going to be held in Mary's new LDS ward building, the local church leaders there were apparently in control of much of what was going to happen. Before the service started, Liz was in her coffin in one of the church's side rooms (called the Relief Society room). Here, visitors were able to see her for the viewing prior to the actual services.

Just as with Erik, it was so sad to see my little girl in that situation, and knowing that she was gone forever. Karl was going to get married in about three weeks, and Lisbeth was going to be one of the bridesmaids at his wedding. Liz was dressed in the bridesmaid's dress she was going to wear. I brought Lisbeth's favorite stuffed animal—the ragged little bear that she called "Hospital"—and placed it in the casket with her. Someone else had put a Mormon Church "Choose the Right" (CTR) ring on her finger. Marit gave Lisbeth the Marine Corps pin that she received upon graduation from boot camp.

In preparing for the funeral service, I asked Lisbeth's brothers and sister to join me in writing final letters to her.

This was a devastating time for my other children. They were suffering a special pain that I couldn't imagine: the premature loss of their sister. Lisbeth was an integral part of their group. These children grew up together. They had a relationship that can only be understood by siblings; children who eat, sleep, and play together on a daily basis. Lisbeth's death affected them profoundly. They lost a part of themselves.

As was the case with Erik, I intended to have these letters read during the service, and then place them in the casket with her. It sickened me to realize that my original intent—when I was starting a family—was to have a tradition of writing special letters to each of my children on their *birthdays*. Instead, I now had a tradition of writing good-bye letters to my children when they died.

Prior to the funeral, when I was sitting in the office of Mary's bishop, I explained to this man the fact that we would be reading these letters aloud, and then place them in the casket at the end of the talk. The bishop said that would not be allowed.

"Why?" I asked, quite astonished. During Erik's service at the funeral home, the pastor had put my letter in the casket after he read it. Nobody had a problem with that.

"Because open caskets are not allowed in the chapel," he replied.

"The casket doesn't have to be open during the service," I said. "It can stay closed. I'll just open the lid far enough to place the letters in with her and close it again."

"That's not allowed."

"Why? What's the reasoning behind that rule?"

"It's just not allowed."

At that point, someone—I don't remember who—came into the office and asked how things were going.

"Not well," I said. "This guy's being a coward. He's not allowing me to put letters into the casket with Liz during the service, and he won't tell me why."

I don't know why I used the word *coward* to describe this bishop at that time. It *was* a somewhat milder term than the several names I *wanted* to call him at that moment. I'm sure this bishop didn't actually know *why* an open casket was not allowed in the chapel section of their building (even for a few seconds); he was likely just following one of the thousands of rules and customs that permeate Mormon Church life—rules that exist without rhyme or reason. The main point in the church is that rules must be unquestioningly obeyed, and he was obeying them. I ended up having to quickly go somewhere to get these letters copied. I placed the original letters in the casket with Lisbeth at the end of the viewing (before they took her to the chapel), and I read from the copies during the service.

Karl's letter:

Lisbeth Clair Skollingsberg, whom I love very much. We have always been so close. You always wanted to be around me, and I loved every minute of it. My friends would come over and you would hurry into the kitchen and make some brownies or cookies. All of my friends loved you. You did whatever you could so we could be together. I was always looking out for you, doing whatever I could to help you, to keep you safe.

We always had such a special bond in life. I love the way you and I got along. You supported me when I knew no one else would. I know that when I went on my mission, it almost tore you apart. You would send me letters telling me that you missed me, and those letters tore me apart. I wanted you to be so happy. You knew that I was doing what was right. When I got home you had grown so much; you were even more beautiful than before, and you were so excited to see me. You had to go home shortly, but I made it up there to visit. We talked and talked and enjoyed each other's company. I would end up sitting next to the fire with you in my lap, and I would just hold you. I was loving to be with you. Soon I had to go again, but I would call you and we would talk. As soon as you heard it was me on the phone, you would immediately want to talk to me. You trusted me and would tell me about your problems and your worries, and just about how your day was.

Finally, after months of waiting, you got to come and stay with me. We both had to fight to make that happen, but we won and we got to spend the last week of your precious life together. We worked hard, I had to move, but we also had a lot of fun. One day, as I was putting my entertainment center together, you read to me for seven hours, even though you didn't want to.

You ate popsicles, lots of them. You would get mad at me because I would wake you up earlier in the morning than you wanted to wake up so I could be with you.

I wanted a bite from one of your popsicles and you didn't want to give me one. So I jumped on you and said I would take a bite out of you instead. You laughed and laughed; you thought that it was so silly. I loved to hear you laugh, to see you smile.

You were such a wonderful girl, and I'm sorry you didn't get to do things you most wanted to do in this life—that is, to get married and have your own little family. It kills me to know all the things you wanted to do you can no longer do. I wish you were still here with me so we could laugh and be happy together again. There's a really huge hole in my heart where you were, Lisbeth, a hole that hopefully can be filled or be lessened by time.

I still talk to you all the time, hoping that you'll answer me. I went to see you that morning and they had your body on that gurney, covered all but your head and shoulders with a red sheet. I talked to you and held your head in my arms. I kissed you and I cried. I whispered things in your ear. I told you how much I missed you and told you to be good and safe.

You wanted so badly to finish the book you were reading so I told you how it ended. I still have a hard time believing that you are gone. I know that it is not a dream, and that makes me sad. Every time I think about you, I cry and I realize that I'll never see you in this life again. I will get to see your cold, lifeless body one more time, and then I'll have memories of you to sustain me. I miss you so much and I love you more than I can express. You are wonderful. I love you.

Marit's letter:

My dear, darling Lisbeth,

I love and miss you so much. You are my little girl, my companion always. Right now, I'm looking at pictures from the only time we went rock climbing together. You are so fearless. You've always been the bravest and most adventurous of all us kids.

I'm so sorry for all the mean things I've ever done to you. I know you've forgiven me—you always did. The last time I talked to you, we argued over who was cuter, Johnny Depp, Vin Diesel, Colin Farrell, or Toby McGuire. I'm still going to have to stick with Vin Diesel.

I know I threatened you with having to graduate with your younger brother because of your grades, but I was only trying to motivate you to pass your classes. Pappa told me that you wanted to be a marine; I know you looked up to me and I wanted to be a good example to you. If only it hadn't been for your asthma, you would have been the best marine ever, so full of energy, motivation, and desire.

You certainly gave us a couple scares in your life with pneumonia and been hospitalized twice for it. Everyone was jealous of the flowers, balloons, and cable TV, but you only wanted to get out so you could run and play again.

I remember teasing you for having to shop for school clothes at the thrift shop because you only had $40 to spend. All you wanted was a shirt, pants, and a skirt. You never wanted much.

Thank you for standing up for me against the family members when I wasn't there to defend myself. You were always so good to me.

You told me you were having fun with Karl, but you weren't eating very well. I wish I could have been able to take care of you.

I congratulated you for getting kicked out of church camp because I did the same thing as you at your age. I just didn't get sent home.

I can't believe you never got to date. I remember your first crush on *Malcom in the Middle*. Now I've lost the chance to hear about your first kiss, date, dance, or even prom. I've always thought of you as my own daughter, and I apologize if I ever seemed overbearing to you. I know I've acted like an overprotective mother.

That was another strength—you loved kids, and they all swarmed around you all the time. I was jealous when Emily's baby, J. J., smiled more for you than for me. You were the queen of all the babysitters. You were fun, creative, full of energy.

You were a little tough one, too. You always had such strong biceps. The muscles were well defined because of the steroids and the cortisone you always had to take for your eczema.

When we used to share a bed, you must have had fighting dreams because you would hit and kick me so much all night long. You never remembered by the next morning, but we laughed about it always. You would fall asleep curled in a ball, but as soon as you would start snoring, you would roll over onto your back so fast that your fist would be heavily dropped on my face. Then you would sleep sprawled out all over the bed. I'd have to keep sliding you back to your half of the bed.

We painted your dresser with teddy bears and hearts.

I will always miss you and I'm sorry for not cherishing every minute we had together. I will keep these memories close to my heart forever.

I love you so much, Lizzy-Bear.

Peder's letter:

Hello Lizzy,

Thank you so much for being you. Thank you for being everybody's baby girl. Thank you for all your sweetness and everything. I'm so sorry it had to turn out like this. You have so many people who love you so much—I love you so much.

I will do everything I can to make you happy. I know that you are happy and want all of us not to be sad, but we're all going to miss you. You're making me anxious to see you again, but I know that we will. Later, I promise that I will make it to the celestial kingdom to be with you. Watch over me until then, my beautiful baby sister.

With all my love, Peder

By the way, thank you for all the comfort you have given me.

Gunnar Roy's letter:

Lizzy, I love you so much. Everyone does. I will miss you, too. You're always so cute and spunky and funny. You can make anyone smile when you wanted to. I remember when we played Jane and Joe together. You would always make it fun.

You're so hard to keep up with. I'm sorry I always tagged along with you and your friends. I looked up to you and loved you with all my heart.

I was the last one to touch you when you were alive, and the last one to talk to you. For that, I am so happy.

With all my love,

Your little brother, Gunnar Roy

After Lisbeth's death, Peder recognized my need for support and comfort, and he moved into my house with me for several weeks so I wouldn't be alone. I'm grateful for this kindness and his presence helped me greatly during that period. All through the coming school year, as well as for the two following years, Gunnar Roy also came and lived with me for his scheduled visitation periods (generally a week at a time). I relished these times when my children were with me because it enabled me to function as a father again—the role which had been my purpose in life.

A few days after the funeral, I received a letter in the mail from a group called Compassionate Friends. The literature that was enclosed described this as a national self-help organization consisting of family members of children who had died (the local chapter apparently scanned newspaper obituaries and sent invitations to those listed as "parents" or "survivors" of recently deceased children). After several weeks, I called one of the numbers given, and I eventually got up the courage to attend a local meeting.

Just as I had needed to talk with someone after Erik died, I also needed a sympathetic ear after Lisbeth's death. The Compasisonate Friends group met this need; there were approximately twenty people at the meeting who were *all* surviving family members (no professional counselors). I was free to share whatever I wanted and to listen to others working through their own grief. Similarly to what had happened with my friend's wife, Suzann, I found this process to be very helpful and theraputic; I needed to speak with people who *knew* and *understood* my feelings, just as I understood theirs. I participated in this group (off and on) for several years, and it was a comfort to do so..

Twenty One

Regret

I hold it true, whate'er befall; I feel it when I sorrow most;
'Tis better to have loved and lost Than never to have loved at all.
—*Alfred, Lord Tennyson*

I have regrets—*many* regrets. If I could have a do-over in my life, I sometimes think I'd probably change 99 percent of the decisions I've made and the things I've done. Occasionally, I feel like I've never done *anything* right in my life—a feeling which often resurfaces during my periods of low self-esteem and depression.

Overall, most of the regrets in my life center on my children. I am *so* sorry for the times that I was angry or impatient with them, and the times I made them sad or caused them to cry. I continue to hurt inside when I remember scolding Erik when he picked up the neighbor's newspaper. I'm filled with guilt when I remember that I made Lisbeth cry when I used rubbing alcohol to clean her scratched and bloodied wrists— that was a horrible thing to do. I even feel sorry for talking Lisbeth into saving some of her money in her bank account when she really wanted to spend it, instead; she should have enjoyed whatever that money could have purchased for her at that moment. I was trying to teach her about money management and how to save for the future, but—in the end—it didn't do her any good sitting in the bank when she died.

Of course, my biggest regrets are related to the circumstances surrounding Erik and Lisbeth's deaths.

I sometimes think about what would have happened if we had *not* stopped for food at that takeout restaurant on the way home from the movie that July evening. We would have arrived at that fateful intersection just a few minutes earlier than we did, and we would have missed that speeding car. Erik would have survived, and many lives would have been changed for the better. In fact—to be perfectly safe—we *should* have stayed home that night and not even gone to the movie. That way, we wouldn't have even been out on the streets at all.

As for Lisbeth, my regret is that I didn't argue more forcefully when Mary said she wanted to take Lisbeth on that camping trip. It wasn't my fault that Mary had not been in Oregon very much that summer and hadn't spent a lot of time with Lisbeth there. Lisbeth was supposed to be with *me*. Perhaps I should've gotten into my car at that time and driven across the state—ahead of Mary and Dan—to physically get Lisbeth myself, to make sure she came home with *me* rather than go on that trip. Mary's record and experience with camping wasn't good; I should have anticipated that there could—or would— be significant problems. I also regret that I didn't even *consider* the possibility that they might go swimming on their camping trip. If I'd known about these plans (or even thought of it), I would have insisted that my children take their life vests with them and told them to make sure they used them.

Sometimes I let my mind reflect on how different things would be if these two precious children had not died when they did. Especially on their birthdays, I think about how old they would have been and what kinds of life experiences they would have had. Occasionally, I meet people who were born in the same years as Erik and Lisbeth. When this happens, I think about what my children would have looked like at these ages, what they would have accomplished, and who they would have met and affected in their personal life journeys. I also wonder what their personalities would have been like; would their individualities have changed much from those I had seen in them when they were children?

Besides these regrets, I also experience sorrow and sadness. I'm not sad for myself; I'm sad for *them*. I'm sad that these two precious little children didn't have a chance to live out their lives.

Little Erik was only two years old when he died. Every day of life was an adventure for him. It was a delight to watch him— *every* day was a day of excitement for him; every moment was a fresh chance to learn new things and to explore this wonderful world around him. His whole future was an open book, just waiting for him to eagerly fill in the pages and color them with marvelous hues as he traveled through life.

Lisbeth was at the age when she had become aware of the multitude of possibilities open to her. She had made great plans and developed expectations for her life. Lisbeth already knew she wanted to marry and have a family. She loved children and enjoyed babysitting, and looked forward to the time when she would have her own family and her own children. More immediately, Lisbeth was in the process of getting her driver's license, and she was looking forward to the freedom and responsibilities that this would bring. Lisbeth had already decided that she was going on to college after high school and would train for a profession, she had recently mentioned the possibility of becoming a teacher. Her future was an open book as well, with all its limitless possibilities and promises.

Two wonderful children, two precious lives, two limitless futures—gone.

Both of these precious lives ended; prematurely and suddenly—without warning.

At the risk of sounding selfish, I also regret that I wasn't able to continue to be Erik and Lisbeth's father, that the time I had with them was too short. I was deprived of years of happiness with each of them.

When Erik and Lisbeth woke up on their individual, fateful days, neither of these children had any idea that that would be their *last* day on Earth. Neither knew that they would not experience another dawn or sunset, that they would never see, hold, or hug their loved ones again after that day. They would not even be able to say good-bye to anybody. Each died with no warning and no preparation.

I am sometimes tortured with thoughts about how my children died. Erik received a blow to the head and was immediately rendered unconscious. Other than the pain he might have felt at the moment of the collision, he likely didn't experience any conscious discomfort during those next few days that he lived. On the other hand, Lisbeth likely experienced panic and horror when she found that she couldn't rise back up to the surface of that river. She was probably terrified for those few minutes when she tried to hold her breath and fight to survive. After two or three minutes of struggling, her lungs literally ached for more oxygen and she was forced to breathe, only to have them painfully fill with water. Finally, unconsciousness mercifully descended, and her emotional terror and physical pain ended. These thoughts haunt me.

Parents are supposed to be teachers for their children. Parents are supposed to draw on and use their own experiences to teach their young children about life. We teach our children how to walk and talk, how to play and share, and how to live well. In the normal order of life, *we* do things first, and our children follow *after* us (and hopefully they learn from watching our mistakes and are able to live better lives than we did). As they grow up, our children watch the relationship we have with our spouses, and they learn what works and what doesn't work so they can decide how to relate to their own partners, if and when they marry. Children watch as their parents struggle with finances or employment, and it helps them to determine their own professions.

Sometimes, however, children become the teachers. In my case, two of my children went through a major life experience before I did. As a parent, I should die before my children do, partly so they can see and learn about this stage of life and help them to decide how to face their own mortality. But Erik and Lisbeth both went through this stage *before* me, and that feels so completely unnatural. They've both already experienced the ultimate life event that I've not yet experienced: death. I highly resent that.

This chapter began with a famous quote from Tennyson. He wrote this as part of a much longer poem in tribute to a very close friend of his who had died. This poem suggests a very valid question: Is it really better to have experienced love—even though the person you loved later dies (causing unspeakable pain)—than to have never experienced this love at all? I have sometimes thought very seriously about this.

Erik's mother, Janet, had told me that her way of coping with his death was to try to forget that he ever lived. That is what she did to try to retain her sanity. Given recent advances in neuroscience, it may be actually possible in the not too distant future to identify, isolate, and permanently remove selected memories in human brains. Perhaps this may not be just science fiction in the future.

I have thought seriously about this. If I was given this option, would I want to have the memories of Erik and Lisbeth erased? Would that be better for me? The answer here is easy: no. I relish the memories of *all* my children too much to ever want to have any of them removed.

Returning to Tennyson's comment, however, I have considered the implied question: Is it really better to have loved someone and then lost him or her to death than to never have loved this person in the first place? Is the pain worth the gain?

Erik had such a short life; he was alive for just over two years and he has been gone now for over thirty years. Are those two years of happiness he provided to me better than the over three decades of daily emotional pain and suffering I've experienced since his death? Lisbeth was alive for almost sixteen years. Is the joy she brought into my life during that time worth the excruciating emotional pain that I have felt—and continue to feel—every day during the eleven-plus years since she died? Is it really possible to quantify and compare these two emotions—to measure the amount of love and the amount of sorrow and place them on a scale? I think about both children (and I miss both of them) many times every day of my life, and it saddens me when I do.

However, I must say that the answer to the question posed—at least for me—is *yes!* I treasure and cherish the lives, the love, and *all* of the moments that I have spent with each and every one of my children, both those who are living and those who have died.

I wholeheartedly agree with Tennyson. As horribly painful as it was—and continues to be—it *is* better to have loved and lost than to have never loved at all.

Twenty Two

Depression

I hate living;
I hope I die soon.
I wish I was never born.
—Author

Everybody experiences depression at different times in their lives—and these depressed moods can last from hours to days to weeks, or even months (and sometimes longer). I believe that I have experienced symptoms of clinically identifiable depression for nearly my entire life.

How does a person become depressed, particularly during childhood (when life is supposed to be exciting and fun)?

An important factor in the development of depression in childhood is the self-concept that is formed as a result of the way the child has been treated by others. When a child has not learned adequate or appropriate coping skills, he perceives that other people's actions and words are actually telling him that he is not appreciated, wanted, or valued. The child can develop the belief that he is worthless. These negative experiences are especially effective when they have been meted out by those who are supposed to love, care for, and cherish the child—his or her own family members.

I believe I was about six (or barely seven) years old when the following event occurred. We were living in our first house (the one that we had moved into after initially arriving in the United States). This house was somewhat close to the city center. (We had moved further out to the suburbs the summer after I turned seven.) There was some sort of theater, arena, or television studio (I don't remember exactly which) in the city center that hosted professional wrestling bouts on Friday nights. Although these shows were broadcast live on television, my father enjoyed watching these matches in person. So, almost every Friday evening, he would announce that he was "going to the fights" and leave. He always went alone.

One evening, I asked my father if I could go with him. He appeared to be surprised at this request, but he agreed. I also wanted to see these fights, and I also wanted to spend time with him.

It was an exciting evening with all the people in the audience screaming and yelling, and the various wrestlers sweating, grunting, and throwing each other around the ring. I enjoyed all the new sights, sounds, and smells. But alas, as the evening drew on and it became quite late, I became tired—*very* tired. I eventually laid down on the bleacher next to my father and fell asleep. When the matches were over, my father woke me and took me home.

Even though I'd slept through part of it, I had enjoyed that evening. When the following Friday rolled around, I asked my father if I could go with him again. He agreed, and we went.

I was again fascinated by the experience, but—as the late evening wore on—I ended up asleep again on the bench next to my father.

The next week, as my father was getting ready to go to the fights again, I ran to get my coat, expecting to go too.

"Why do you want to go?" my father asked. "All you do is sleep anyway!" I was surprised at the way he spat out the words.

I felt crushed, and I put away my coat. I didn't go with him that night, and I never again asked to go to the fights. Perhaps my father just wanted some time to be alone, and he was certainly entitled to that. But—at my young age—I felt that he was teaching me that I wasn't wanted and that I was a nuisance. That was the lesson that I learned all too well.

Children who live with depressed parents are more prone to experience significant depression themselves. Over the years, I discovered that both of my parents suffered severe depression. They were obviously not happy or satisfied with their lives, with each other, or with their children. They both seemed to have basically two emotional states: they were either "in neutral" with their emotions (just plodding along, going through the daily, boring mechanics of life), or they were irritated and angry. More often than not, it was the latter. I really don't recall ever seeing either of my parents actually being *happy* with each other (or with us children) or experiencing real *joy* for any significant amount of time. They would laugh occasionally, but they were basically not happy people.

Nevertheless, I was still surprised—and somewhat shocked—when each of my parents separately made statements to me that indicated the depths of their own depression.

When I was probably fifteen or sixteen years old, my mother and I were having a disagreement about something (which apparently occurred often). There was no yelling or screaming this time, but at one point, my mother looked at me squarely in the eyes and said (with very strong emotion), "Every night, I pray to God that I *never* wake up in the morning!" I was left speechless (and that statement put an end to *that* argument). Later, upon reflection, I suspected that my mother had probably uttered this same prayer nightly for many years.

Several years ago, my father told me about an incident that occurred in the past. I was probably attending the university when this happened, and I was not aware of these events at that time. There had been various degrees of animosity between my father and my middle brother for many years, and their acrimony became almost legendary. There was often shouting and arguing between the two, and over the years, this mutual hostility was occasionally expressed through physical confrontations. Apparently, during one Sunday morning while our father was at a church priesthood meeting, my middle brother (who was then in his mid-twenties) had made some threats that he wanted to—or that he was going to—*kill* our father. Our mother evidently believed these threats were credible, so she telephoned the bishop at our church and asked him to warn our father. My father said that the bishop pulled him out from the Priesthood meeting room and informed him about the threats my brother was making. He advised my father to *not* go home because "your life is in danger."

When my father recounted this story to me, he said, "Of course, I left right then and went home." However, my brother had apparently left their house before he arrived. When I asked my father why he went home to confront someone who was threatening to kill him, he said that he wasn't going to be afraid of his son. Then he added, "Besides, if he would have killed me, he would be doing me a favor!" Upon reflection, I believe that my father subscribed to this sentiment—that he would be better off dead than alive—for most of his life.

These declarations by my parents both surprised and somewhat stunned me when I first heard them, but unfortunately I now understand and *know* these feelings all too well myself.

Besides being a product of how one is treated by others (such as being made to feel unloved, unwanted, and worthless) and having been influenced by being raised and living with severely depressed caregivers, there is also a degree of genetic connection between parents and their children regarding depression—a genetically based predisposition or propensity for developing depression across succeeding generations.

I once told my family physician during an office visit that I believe that I was somehow "hardwired" for depression—that it seemed to be my natural mental state. I had based that conclusion on several factors. Over my lifetime, I've noticed that—among all the different personalities I had encountered in this world—there are some people who have an optimistic, gregarious, and bubbly personality. They are very social, make friends easily, and tend to see the best in any given situation. After carefully observing these certain individuals over the years, I came to the conclusion that such an outgoing and sociable personality was likely not merely the result of *learned* behaviors, but rather that these people were likely *born* with the propensity to develop many of these traits—that is, they appear to be hardwired to some degree to be the way they were.

As parents, we see that our children seem to be born with their own unique personalities. How else can one explain the widely varying personality types that sometimes occur among children who are raised together under similar conditions within the same family? Similarly, I think that those who are extremely shy, withdrawn, and introverted—and those who are almost continuously sad and depressed—could have become that way at least partly through some degree of having been hardwired to be so at birth, through the genetic jumble of their DNA.

Over the years, I have tried various types of antidepressant medications, as prescribed by doctors. While on these medications, I noted a slight decrease in the depth of my depression, but none of them seemed to make large differences in alleviating my depressive thoughts and feelings altogether. Perhaps I was expecting too much, and maybe I was looking for some sort of "happy pill," but I was disappointed that these medications didn't automatically change my depressive emotions to feelings of happiness and joy (such as portrayed in the *Valley of the Dolls* film).

My physician disagreed with my hardwired depression analogy, saying that I hadn't tried all of the different available medications yet (I did note, however, that this particular physician himself seemed to be one of the more optimistic, gregarious individuals I mentioned earlier).

When I was a young child, I was acutely aware of my own pervasive sadness. However, I just thought: *That's the way life is.* I didn't know anything else; that was my reality. I could recognize times when other children felt sad—I could identify with that emotion, and I knew how they felt. But I didn't fully understand how others felt when they were happy and enjoying life. Of course, there were times when I too would laugh and take joy in life, but these moments seemed to be so fleeting—they really didn't last long—and I soon reverted back to my unrelenting gloom.

There were a couple of instances during my late childhood and preteen years when I made what could be called "cries for help" for my depression. I recognized my sadness, and I yearned for some help in alleviating these oppressive feelings.

When I was about ten years old, I developed the idea that nobody in my family loved me, nobody wanted me, and nobody would even care if I just disappeared. I convinced myself of this. One Saturday, I came up with a plan to test this theory. I went into the closet of the bedroom I shared with my middle brother, crouched down on the floor of the closet, and covered myself with a few shirts and other pieces of clothing that were always littering the floor of our bedrooms and closets. Then I waited and listened. I wanted to see how long it would take before someone—anyone—noticed I was missing.

One hour passed. Nothing. I dozed off. When I woke up, I saw that a second hour had gone by. Then a third. I listened to the everyday sounds of the comings and goings of my family members, and there was not a peep about me from any of them. My theory was being proven correct. Finally, after about four hours, my mother did begin asking about me. Nobody knew anything, and the subject was dropped. About thirty minutes later, she asked again. Again, nothing.

When about five hours had passed, my mother finally directed everyone to look throughout the house for me. A search was mounted, all the rooms were checked and someone even looked in my closeted hiding place—but I was nowhere to be found (I had camouflaged myself well). A half hour later, a second search of the house was launched, and my hiding place was finally discovered by my brother. As I came out of the closet, my mother asked why I was in there, why I was hiding.

"I wanted to see if anyone would ever notice I was gone," I replied, quite truthfully.

My parents dismissed this as a silly game I was playing, and more evidence that I was either crazy or stupid. They didn't see it as any indication or signal that I felt unloved or that I was depressed.

The second cry for help occurred a few years later. During a particularly sad and depressing time, a period when I *hated* my life, I wrote—in large block letters—"WHY WAS I BORN?" on a sheet of notebook paper. I didn't tear up that paper or throw it away; instead, I had left it among a pile of other loose papers and homework in my room (perhaps I left it as a subconscious plea for help). A couple of days later, my mother found this paper and asked me about it. I acknowledged that I had written it. Instead of recognizing this as a sign of depression, my mother launched into a stern lecture about the Mormon Church's Plan of Salvation doctrine: "You were born so that you could have a body, and so you can be tried in this life," she began. "And if you are able to live the gospel and follow the commandments on this Earth, you will be able to return to our heavenly Father and have eternal life..." and so on and so on. She seemed perturbed at having to explain all this to me again when I should have learned and memorized it from my seemingly never ending church attendance. I just nodded as she went on with her lecture. She didn't get it.

Over the years, my depression seemed to grow—day to day, year after year, decade upon decade. My propensity for depression, my hardwired brain, and my devastating life experiences all combined to create a depth of depression that occasionally surprised even me.

These were distressing periods of my life when I felt totally worthless, when I couldn't be around other people because I didn't want others to be subjected to me; I didn't even want to others to have to *look* at me. At these times, I literally hated myself. I *hated* living, I hated existence itself, and I even resented having been born (an event that I had no control over).

These exceptionally brutal feelings would usually last for periods of time ranging from a few hours to several days (and occasionally longer). These very disturbing feelings also seemed to be cyclical; they came, stayed, and left, only to inevitably return perhaps days, weeks, or even a month or two later. But they always *did* return.

As a result of this ongoing and destructive depression, I eventually created three self-talk statements that reflected my feelings during those periods: *I hate living. I hope I die soon. I wish I was never born.*

These statements soon became a barometer of my feelings at any particular moment. If I was having a particularly stressful time during one of my "down" cycles, I might repeat one or more of these statements in my mind, or by whispering or mumbling to myself. This might occur literally *hundreds* of times (or even more) throughout the day. If the day was going all right and there were no unexpected stressors, these words might only be uttered maybe a total of a dozen times or less.

Perhaps a reader may ask, "If you hate life so much, why don't you just end it? Why prolong your misery?"

The ultimate expression of deep depression, of the feelings of being unloved, unwanted, and a burden to others, is self-destruction—suicide. I admit that I have thought about this, and I have seriously considered taking this route in the past. Two such occasions occurred after my second divorce (but before Lisbeth's death), when I seemed mired in the lowest points of some of my down cycles.

In one such instance, I had been traveling overseas, and I was staying in a hotel in St. Petersburg, Russia. My room was on the fourth floor, which happened to be the top floor of that hotel. The room's window opened wide, and I therefore had complete access to the outside. It was winter, and I remember looking down at the dark, ice-covered sidewalk below. It was *very* cold—perhaps minus five degrees Fahrenheit. I felt a hopelessness that was as dark as that wintry night sky, and I *really* wanted relief—to escape life.

I sat on the window sill, looking out. I carefully considered all of the variables I could think of: *How far was it down to the street? Was this distance enough to ensure death if I jumped out? The fall wouldn't last long, just a second or two.* Then I thought about what would happen if I was successful and I died in that far-off place: *Would my family be responsible for taking my body back to the United States? They can't afford this, and they should just leave my body here. But would they do that? What would that cost?* Being dead, I would have no control over those decisions. *Maybe they would feel the need to retrieve my body, and they might go into debt to do that. That wouldn't be good.* Then I thought about a possible alternative fate that might occur when I jumped out that window: *What if the distance isn't enough to make certain I'll die when I hit the ground? Maybe four stories isn't high enough; maybe I'd just be injured instead. What would happen then? Would I be paralyzed? A quadriplegic? Brain damaged? Maybe I would then have to spend the rest of my already miserable life with paralysis or severe brain damage. Is that what I want? Is that an option?*

After considering all of these questions and alternative scenarios for about fifteen minutes, I closed the window and sat back down on the bed, shivering, waiting for the room to warm up again. I had decided against suicide for that moment. I wondered how the events of that evening might have been very different if I had by chance checked into a hotel that had many more floors and I had a higher room.

My second serious brush with suicide also involved seemingly insurmountable feelings and emotions. I was living alone, and I felt abandoned by my family and my children, and again I was wallowing in the bottom of my dark, emotional pit. In my mind, I was convinced that no one loved me, no one cared about me, and that I was an irritant and an annoyance to others—especially to my children. My children rarely called me, and when I telephoned them, they often sounded like they were preoccupied with something (it seemed that I somehow always called during one of their favorite television programs or they had been in the middle of a video game or when they were on their way out the door to do something). I was likely mistaken, but in my mind, I told myself that they were not happy to hear from me.

Another major factor that occurred at about this time was that my fiftieth birthday had recently come … and gone, and I felt that *nobody cared*. I sat there in my empty apartment, thinking back to *my* father's fiftieth birthday. On that occasion, my mother had rallied all us children together and planned a surprise birthday party for our father. We made a banner that read, "Happy Half Century!" My mother made a cake, and she bought a gift. She even arranged to have my father's brother and his family come over to our house to participate in the festivities (even though both familes lived in the same city, a visit from them was a rare occurrence).

My father had received an elaborate fiftieth birthday celebration from *his* family, and here I was, sitting alone, wallowing in self-pity.

I saw that there was a basic difference between me and my father. My father had not divorced my mother, and his family was still intact, while Mary and I *had* divorced, and our family was torn apart. I felt like I was only getting what I deserved. It was then that I entered a stage in the self-destructive process that was frightening.

From my studies, I had learned that thoughts about suicide are often associated with feelings of being unloved, unwanted, and a perception that one is a nuisance to others—a sense that people around them (and in fact the whole world) would be better off if they were dead. Also, those contemplating suicide are frequently facing what are perceived to be insurmountable problems in one or more other aspects of their lives. These life problems might include a relationship that has gone badly (or has ended) or serious financial difficulties. Sometimes people come to this stage because they face possible criminal charges for something they've done (or been accused of). These are all viewed by the despondent individual as insurmountable problems.

With the feelings of worthlessness—and overwhelming troubles and tribulations—the suicidal person feels mentally and emotionally tortured. This is a very real pain, and at some point, he/she may decide that there is only *one* action that offers a seemingly simple and complete solution: death, nonexistence.

I knew that this is an *extremely* dangerous point. The person makes the decision that death is the only way to relieve themselves from their torment, agony, and pain and that all their problems will vanish upon their demise. The knowledge that this unbearable suffering can end *soon*, actually brings a feeling of peace to the individual.

That night in my apartment, I felt that peace—that euphoria—that comes with the knowledge and certainty that everything will soon be better, that all my problems would be solved and gone, and that the devastating pain will finally end. I realized that I was just minutes away from death.

It frightened me.

I can't remember exactly what my self-destruction plan was, but at that point, I made a conscious effort to do *nothing* that would facilitate my death. I didn't look for my gun, or search out something to use to hang myself with. I didn't go to the kitchen to get a carving knife. I forced myself to just sit there, in that living room, and do *nothing*. After many minutes, the peace and elation I had felt earlier (when I had decided to die) eventually subsided, and all of the sorrow and the problems had reappeared. The pain returned, and things were "normal" again.

Many children—and some adults—look on each new day as another opportunity to see what life has to offer—to experience the myriad of adventures that await them. Even as a child, however, I mostly *dreaded* each new day; I was convinced that every day presented new problems and more difficulties— these were things that I had to *endure*, not enjoy. As I became older, the number and magnitude of these problems and difficulties only grew larger, year after year. Eventually, I came up with a brief statement that quite clearly described my attitude and philosophy toward life:

Life: You're born, you suffer, you die.

At first, this appeared to me to be morbidly pessimistic and an indication of the depth of my lifelong depression. However, I have since discovered that there are others who have either a similar attitude or who are at least acquainted with this philosophy.

I once watched a documentary program on television in which the former USSR leader Mikhail Gorbachev related a story about a Russian czar's search for the meaning of life. This czar assembled many of his country's most brilliant intellectuals and philosophers to tackle this question. After initially producing a multivolume academic study on the meaning of life, the czar repeatedly requested significant editing and shortening of this information. They returned with a single, thick book of life's meaning, which they presented to the czar. He demanded another abridgement, and then another. In the end, these scholars finally developed a single sentence that reflected the bare essence of their studies (which was very similar to what I had developed on my own): "One is born, one suffers, and then one dies." When I heard this story, I imagined that many Russians must be as fatalistic and as depressed as I was.

There are others who have used similar phrases as well. I found that the contemporary poet and essayist Joseph Epstein wrote a poem titled: "All men and women are born, live, suffer, and die." The Christian evangelist Billy Graham also used this phrase as a topic for one of his sermons, the title of which begins with "You're born. You suffer. You die" (the rest of the sermon's title reads, "Fortunately, there's a loophole").

In any event, it was enlightening to discover that my pessimistic outlook on life was not *entirely* unique; others were at least aware of the fundamental nature of this attitude.

Although I experience this depression—and have done so for essentially my entire life—I found a couple of ways in which I could try to control the effect of this depression on myself and others around me.

When I was young (about twelve or so), I developed an interest in radios and electronics (after my oldest brother became an amateur radio operator—a "ham"). I quickly learned how to build crystal radio sets. These are simple radio receivers that do not use batteries and are powered only by the strength of the radio signals sent out from nearby radio stations (that way, I didn't have to ask my parents for money to buy batteries). I built and experimented with these radios, and I would often lie in bed at night, listening to the music from these stations through a single earphone. I discovered that I found comfort in music, and I would often fall asleep while listening to this simple receiver. It became a small, positive experience in my otherwise cheerless days.

A few years later, I got a paper route and I was able to afford to buy my own batteries. I bought a small transistor radio that was capable of receiving more stations from longer distances. Now I was able to listen to more types of wonderful music. After that, I used money that I earned from part-time jobs to buy a record player and records. I even joined a record club—ordering a number of albums upon enrollment and promising to purchase more throughout the following year.

I found that music gave me momentary escape from the dreariness of my life. For two or three minutes, each song let me live vicariously in another reality, in a different world. My life in this imaginary world was much better than the life I was living in my real world. Through music, I could imagine that I was in a relationship with someone, I could actually be in love, and someone loved me back. I could feel that I was worth something; I was valued by *someone*. The music genre didn't matter—it could be a country and western ballad or a rock 'n' roll song—I put myself into the music and experienced new emotions: friendship, tenderness, affection, and love; these were feelings that I did not have in my daily life. And, because of my extreme shyness and difficulty in relating to others, I believe I used these songs as a crutch so I didn't have to go out and try to experience these emotions in real life, with real people. It was much safer to just imagine.

One could say that I was fortunate in this endeavor, because the late 1950s and the entire 1960s were a veritable gold mine for such music—a treasure trove of songs into which I could easily get lost. I vicariously experienced feelings of love in "Summer Wine" by Nancy Sinatra and Lee Hazelwood, "Calendar Girl" by Neil Sedaka, "For Your Love" by The Yardbirds, and "You Were on My Mind" by We Five, as well the sadness of lost love, such as in "Crying" and "Only the Lonely" by Roy Orbison and "Cry Like a Baby" by The Box Tops.

I also seemed drawn to some songs that expressed the difficulties and tragedy of life, such as "El Paso" by Marty Robbins, "Big Bad John" by Jimmy Dean, and especially "Elusive Dreams" by Sinatra and Hazelwood.

Some songs painted a picture of a life I *yearned* to have—a life that was only possible in a dream world, because I knew I would never be able to actually live it. These songs included "Greenfields," by the Brothers Four; "Try to Remember (the Kind of September)," by the Sandpipers; and "A Home in the Meadow," by Debbie Reynolds, from the movie *How the West Was Won.*

I see now that some of the songs I connected with in my early teen years were somewhat prophetic and foreshadowed events that would occur in my own future, such as "Leader of the Pack," by the Shangri-Las (involving a motorcycle accident, which I later experienced when I was sixteen); J. Frank Wilson and the Cavaliers' version of "Last Kiss" (concerning losing a loved one in a traffic accident); and "Running Bear" (relating to the death of a girl due to drowning).

I could go on and on, page after page, listing all of the songs and music from that era and from that point in my life that significantly affected me—that I used to try to experience (to some degree, at least) the missing emotions of my life. But I'll stop here.

When I listen to this music now, it's a bittersweet experience. On the one hand, I enjoy this music very much and love listening to it; there was some *damn* good music in those days. On the other hand, these songs also bring me back—emotionally—to that time when I was a child and a teenager, those years when I used this music to escape my daily sadness, when I could pretend that I was not alone, and that I had someone to love (and I was loved in return). These songs reawaken those years and trigger feelings of nostalgia and sentimentalism.

My depression is still present. I've accepted the fact that it's a part of my everyday life and always will be; it'll never go away. But I've learned to live with this albatross, and I've tried to function day by day with it, constantly trying not to let its weight overwhelm me.

There are several activities and practices that I have used to try to combat the effects of depression.

As I've mentioned, I have used medication to help keep me out of the seemingly bottomless depths of the severe depressive episodes that occasionally envelope me. It often takes time and effort to locate a medication that will be most effective. I also realize that medication alone cannot solve the problem, and other means must also be employed.

One activity that I use to fight depression is just that: *activity*. I have found (and research supports this finding) that excercise helps alleviate some depressive symptoms. Personally, I prefer to take walks—long walks—as opposed to a gym workout. I often use this method when I am on vacation (where I don't have a car to get around in and I *have* to walk).

I have also seen that the main deterrent to this method is *motivation*—when I'm depressed I don't *want* to go out and exercise, I don't *want* to do anything (many times, I don't even want to get out of bed). A way I combat this is to make a weekly schedule of my activities (that includes exercise), and then commit to sticking to this schedule. If my schedule says "Saturday afternoon: 3:00 pm – walk 20 minutes," then—at 3:00 pm on Saturday afternoon—*I head out the door*, walk ten minutes in one direction, and then turn around and walk back to my starting point. I have found that—for me—this is the best way to get things done: by dedicating and setting aside specific times for various activites, and then following through.

It's one way I use to keep going, especially when my depression tells me I don't want to.

Another technique I use that is effective in combating depression is to *keep busy*. It generally doesn't matter so much what the activity is, but it's important I do *something* to fill my time (such as working at my job, engaging in one of my hobbies, meeting with friends, etc.). As part of keeping busy, sometimes I learn something new. For example, in order to maintain my teaching credentials, I must take courses equal to six semesters' credit from an accredited college or university every five years. This gives me the "excuse" to keep busy by learning, studying, and interacting with other people, thus lessening some of my depressive symptoms. The key here is that by keeping busy, I do not have the time to think about myself and how difficult life is.

When I feel overwhelmed by my problems—when life seems too much to bear—I have used another technique to help me cope: I make a list of all of the problems and troubles that I am experiencing at that moment (ranging all the way from major life issues to minor things that are getting under my skin). This list starts rather quickly, and I soon have a lengthy inventory of the many things that are truly bothering me. Once this list is made, I then divide these problems into two columns: those issues that I can do something about (things that I can fix), and those that I have no control over. Temporarily ignoring the list of concerns that I cannot control, I turn my attention to the column of things I *can* do something about. This quickly becomes a to-do list, and I start tackling the itemized items; some I can solve and some I can only partially set right, but I at least do something to help solve or fix each problem. This keeps me busy doing something constructive, and—as each issue is solved or moderated—part of the stress, worry, and anxiety that I am experiencing is decreased. I no longer feel so overwhelmed by my problems.

I have also sought out professional assistance to help combat depression. I've asked for referrals from colleagues and my physcian, and I've followed up on their recommendations. I've found that behavioral-cognitive therapy can be quite useful in helping me to gain a new, nondestructive way of looking and thinking about problems.

If my level of depression is so low that I think suicide may be an answer, I have been able to recognize these symptoms and to realize and acknowledge the danger. At those times, I have been able to work through these feelings. However, this can take great effort, and sometimes I've needed the help of others. I have found, however, that it is often difficult for me to accept help at those times.

During periods of exceptional hopelessness, I've learned to look forward; I say to myself, *I can get through this.* Sometimes, this will be one day at a time (*I can survive until tomorrow*), or even one hour at a time (*I can make it for another hour*), but I do try to look forward. Once that hour or that day has passed—and I've survived—I see that I can make it through *another* hour or *another* day. I go through this process as long and as often as it takes until the deep depressive feelings eventually pass.

I have also made a deliberate effort to create and build a *positive* side to my life in order to try to undo some of the sadness I have inside me (as well as the sadness I sometimes see in people around me). In doing so, this has become an attempt to define for myself a new purpose—a new *mission*—in my life. The specific efforts I've used are described in the following chapter.

Twenty Three

Laughter

When the voices of children are heard on the green,
And laughing is heard on the hill,
My heart is at rest within my breast,
And everything else is still.
—William Blake

I have worked in the field of education for nearly my entire adult life; I have been a special education teacher, a "regular" education teacher, and a school psychologist. Over these decades, I have become acquainted with literally thousands of students, met many of their parents, and occasionally had a glimpse into their home lives. I've seen how these children interact with each other, with the staff members of their schools, and I've had a glimpse of their relationships with their parents. I've watched as these children have experienced good times and bad, as they've played and fought, and as they've laughed and cried.

I have seen that *all* children go through times when they struggle and endure great difficulties. It may be because of problems with classmates (they might have just lost a friend, been rejected by others, or are being bullied by one or more other children). They may have difficulties with teachers or others in authority at the school (there can be personality conflicts or other problems with adults), or the children may have difficulties with their classwork (they might not understand the work, find it's too hard for them, or they just don't want to do it). Sometimes, children come to school with their minds and emotions already in disarray because of something happening either in their homes or elsewhere in the community.

In meetings with parents, I've sometimes witnessed the interaction between them and their children. These ranged all the way from kind and loving relationships to real abuse. Some parents did not even attempt to hide their disrespect or anger toward their children.

In one case, I was meeting with a classroom teacher and a parent in an otherwise empty classroom, while the mother's eight-year-old son—the subject of this meeting—was sitting at a nearby desk, drawing on a piece of paper. During our conversation, the mother twice referred to her son as "a piece of shit." Both times this happened, I quickly glanced over to the child (who surely had heard this), and saw no reaction—he just kept on with his drawing. This indicated to me that this was not anything new for this boy; he most certainly had heard this appellation many times before. Unfortunately (from my own childhood experiences), I had an idea of the emotional harm that this was likely doing to that young boy—that his own mother commonly talked to him (and about him) in such a manner. I could have spoken up and informed this mother of the inappropriateness of her comments and the potential harm her words were having on her son, but I remained silent. I had learned—from administrators at different public schools I had previously worked in—that we were never to criticize or question a mother's or father's parenting skills (or lack thereof) during any meetings we had with them.

I've seen children in school who have major emotional and behavioral problems due to depression, significant anxiety disorders, and anger control issues. There are children who have critical health and physical problems, such as severe allergies, asthma, and other childhood diseases and disorders. Also, there are those children who are hurting because they are hungry much of the time.

Childhood isn't always a pleasant time. Too often, childhood is a *hard* time of life. *Damn* hard. Many times, there is an overabundance of difficulties and struggles that children endure—and it breaks my heart. I can't stand to see a child suffer, and I hate to hear a child cry.

But what can *I* do about all this? What can *I* do about the impossible task of ending childhood suffering? I'm not an omniscient, omnipotent god—I'm just one person.

Gradually, over the years of working with and around children, I realized that there *was* something I could do (and it was something I found I was already doing occasionally at my work).

I knew I couldn't end childhood suffering, and I couldn't remove the torments and problems in their lives (however much I wished I could). But I found that there was a way that I *could* make just one moment in their lives a little better—I *could* help remove, for a few seconds, some of the mental or physical pain they were experiencing.

I could do this by making the child *laugh.*

When a child laughs, he/she forgets—for just that moment—that they are depressed, sad, anxious, fearful, angry, in pain, or hungry. For that second or two, life is OK, life is good, life is worth living. When a child laughs, that child is experiencing pleasure and joy.

Intuitively, I knew that children's laughter was a good thing, and there have also been many studies that have supported this conclusion. Laughter—*any* humor—has been found to cause an increase in the levels of endorphins and dopamine in the brain ("feel good" neurotransmitters). Laughter reduces levels of stress, depression, anxiety, and tension while boosting the child's mood, self-esteem, optimism, and energy.

But *I* decided to make children laugh because, when they did, I noticed their eyes light up, I saw their faces form beautiful smiles, and I heard the wonderful sounds of their chuckles and giggles. It's a marvelous event.

I came to realize that the sound of a child's laugh was one of the most wonderful sounds in the world. And I wanted to hear as much of this laughter as I could.

So, my quest—my *mission* in life—became: Make a child laugh, every day. I even formalized this objective by making myself a little sign that I kept privately in my office: "Make a Child Laugh Today."

This was simple, and it was feasible. I already usually joked and played with the children whom I saw when I interacted with them at school (usually when they were subjects of various assessments and evaluations I was conducting with them). After an hour-long test in my office, we would play a couple of quick games of tic-tac-toe or Connect Four, or I had a joke or two for them. I also attempted to extend this practice to any and all children in the school; I wanted them *all* to laugh.

Besides those children who might be experiencing short- or long-term emotional or physical pain, I also knew—all too well—that some children will not have the chance to live out their full childhoods, that a few children will die before reaching adulthood, or even adolescence. We don't know who these children will be. For example, a couple of years after I had worked with one ten-year-old boy as his special education teacher, I learned that he had been diagnosed with Hodgkin's disease, and he passed away the following year. For *these* children, especially, I thought that additional moments of laughter would be particularly touching—that their short lives deserved at least a little more brightness, happiness, and laughter—and I wanted to at least do that for them.

By implementing this goal, I was not only helping the children around me for those few moments, I was also doing it for my own children. Each time I made a child laugh, I thought that my little Erik and my precious Lisbeth would be pleased—they would be proud of me. I did it in *their* remembrance, to honor the memory of my dear children who did not have a chance to live out their own childhoods.

So, exactly how did I go about trying to accomplish this task to make a child (or children) laugh? Over the years, I actually developed several techniques and "routines" that I regularly used to accomplish this goal.

The most basic technique I used was to act silly. As a school psychologist, I would often go into a classroom and ask for a particular student—who was to receive an individual assessment—to accompany me to my office. Once we left the classroom, the fun would begin. I would chat with the student while we walked down the hall. If there was a pillar or a door post in the hallway, I would space my steps so that I would run into the post while I was talking. Upon contact with the pole, I would then be startled (as was the child). I would ask questions like, "How did that get there? Did you put that there? Who put that there? Isn't that dangerous to have a post right in the middle of the hall where people could run into it?" Most of the children would laugh at this, and some would then help direct me as we continued down the hall to make sure I didn't run into any more posts. Apparently, I got very good at this, and it looked realistic. Occasionaly, another staff member walking nearby would see me run into the post and ask if I was all right, thinking that I was seriously hurt. I would later talk with that staff member and explain what I was doing (being silly for the child's benefit), but I added, "If you see me running into posts when I'm *not* with a student, then please do help me, because then something *is* wrong."

Another silly tactic was trying to open doors when I was with a student. If we came to a door that opened by pushing it outward, I would try to pull on the doorknob instead. When it didn't open, I would ask, "What happened to this door? It must be locked. Who locked it? Did *you* lock it? It was open earlier!" The student would usually look up at me with a smile on his or her face. After a couple of more attempts on my part, the student would then push open the door for me. "How did you do that?" I'd ask. At the next door, I would try pushing open the door (if it was a pull-open door), and complain that *this* door was also locked. By this time, the child was usually laughing while he or she pulled the door open. I would then ask with frustration, "How do you know how to do that? How do you know if you're supposed to *push* or *pull* the door to get it open?" After the assessments in my office were completed and it was time to return the child to the classroom, I also "forgot" which way to open my own office door, and the student would laughingly assist me yet again. As the child opened my door for me, I would thank them profusely, adding, "I have so much trouble with this door. You know, sometimes it takes me ten minutes to get out of my office!" Almost invariably this would lead to more laughter. Again, this silliness would bring on different reactions from the other school staff members who had their offices near mine. They eventually realized that I was not really door challenged; I was just being silly and strange. And once I returned the child to the classroom, he or she often had to tell the teacher about their recent adventure with "that silly man."

Walking down the halls of a busy elementary school often presented more opportunities to elicit laughter from the children. In a medium-to-large school, groups of students are often seen walking to or from various classes and activities (such as gym, music, lunch, recess, bus lines, etc.). In order to maintain an orderly transition, the teachers often have the students walk with their hands clasped together or their arms folded. However, if I was walking down the hall in the opposite direction, I would sometimes hold my hand up so as to elicit a "high five." Some students would respond and slap my hand, while others completely obeyed their teacher's previous instructions and kept their hands clasped or arms folded. This also led to some giggling among the ranks of passing students. This also probably irritated and annoyed some of the classroom teachers, but none of them ever expressed their displeasure with me concerning this practice (not directly, anyway).

Sometimes, I was able to take advantage of impromptu situations. Once, when I was walking down the school hallway (alone, this time), I saw that there were students from a second-grade classroom lined up outside of the music classroom door, waiting for another class of children in the room to finish up and leave. While they were waiting, their teacher stood facing them, keeping the children occupied by having them copy semaphore-like signals she was making with her arms. I quietly walked up to about two feet behind the teacher, where the students could see me, but the teacher could not. I then proceeded to make my own arm signals that did not correspond to the teacher's arm signals. Some of the students followed *my* arm movements, while others continued following their teacher's. When I started moving my arms up and down like I was flapping my wings, most of the children did the same, and general laughter broke out. The teacher then turned around and saw me, and I pretended to be caught red-handed and skulked away with my head down, like a naughty boy. The children laughed again, louder. I was glad that the teacher took it well; she said, "We're going to miss Dr. Skollingsberg when he leaves" (I was scheduled to retire at the end of that year).

I became so serious and so driven regarding this goal of making children laugh that I even developed a comedy routine that I used for several years in the different schools I worked in. Using Abbott and Costello's famous *Who's on First?* routine for inspiration, I made my own classroom "reading test." With the teacher's permission, I scheduled a five- to eight-minute session with the class (this usually worked best with students in second through fifth grades). When I arrived in the classroom, the teacher would introduce me by name, and the students would all be seated quietly at their desks, not really knowing what to expect. The following is the general script that I usually followed:

"Good morning. As your teacher said, I'm the school psychologist here. That means that I sometimes take students out for testing once in a while, and I see that some of the students that I've tested in the past are here in this class. But today, I'd like to give a short reading test to the *entire* class." This statement might be followed by either enthusiasm or moans from the children.

"Let's begin."

I write the word *where* on the board in large letters.

I then choose a student at random and ask, "Could you please read this word for me?"

"Where," the student answers.

I look at the board, point to the word, and say, "What do you mean, 'Where?' It's right there. Please read this word."

At this point, many of the students usually realize that this is a game, and that's when the fun begins.

"The word is *where*" is the usual response.

"The word is right *there*," I reply, drawing a circle around the word. "Can't you see it?"

I then pick out another student, and ask him or her to read the word.

"Where!" the student shouts.

"There!" I reply. "It's the word in the circle!"

By this time, virtually all of the students are laughing and enjoying the show. I walk to the back of the room and pick out a student in the last row. I ask, "Can you see that word on the board?"

"Yes."

"The one in the circle?"

"Yes."

"Good," I say. I then return to the front of the room and ask that back-row student to now read the word.

The student says, "Where!"

"Right *here!*" I say, pointing to the board and acting very frustrated. "You *said* you could see it!"

At this point, I'll ask the entire class, "Could *everybody* please read this word?"

"Where!" they all shout.

I then turn to the classroom teacher and say, "I think we need to get the school nurse in here and do vision testing for all these kids. They seem to have a hard time seeing the board!"

Acting somewhat irritated, I then say, "Well, let's go on to the next word." I write the word *what* on the board and choose another student to read it.

"What," the child says.

"Please read this word!" I say, with more volume.

"What!" responds the student.

"Can you hear me?" I ask, acting like I'm shouting.

"Yes!" comes the reply.

"Then *please* read this word!"

"What!"

This same procedure is then tried with a couple of other students, and I act flabbergasted that no one seems to be able to hear me.

Turning to all of the students again, I ask, "Could *everybody* please read this word?"

"*What!*" they all shout.

I look at the classroom teacher again and say, "I think we need to get these students' hearing tested as well!"

The next word I write is *when*.

Picking out yet another student, I point to the word and ask, "Please read this word."

"When."

"Right now."

"When."

"As soon as I point to it."

"When!"

"Right when I touch the word with my finger, I want you to read it," I say. "Will you do that?"

"Yes."

I then slowly bring my finger to the board, and the child shouts, "When!"

"When I touch it!" I respond, frustrated.

Again, this process is tried with a few other children, and I always act flustered at their responses.

I again turn to all the students and ask them all to read the word. As I bring my finger to the board, they all shout, "When!"

After erasing that word, I next write, *who*.

Pointing to another student, I ask, "Could you please read this word?"

"Who," answers the child.

"You," I say, pointing to him or her.

"Who!"

"You! That's who!"

"Who!"

I point out another student in the class, and ask her name. She tells me her name (let's say it's Susan).

"OK, Susan. Would you please read this word?"

"Who!"

"You!" I say. "Susan! *You're* the one I'd like to read this word."

"Who!" she shouts.

Again—after a few other attempts with individual students—the entire class is asked to read the word.

"*Who!*" they all shout.

"*All* of you!" I respond.

Again, I display frustration as I write another word on the board: *why*. Pointing out yet another student, I ask, "Would you please read this word?"

"Why."

"Because I want you to."

"Why."

"Because it's your turn!"

"Why!"

"Because this is a reading test and we're all reading these words and it's your turn, so *please* read this word," I plead.

"Why!"

After further attempts with other students, I turn to the class. "OK. Would *everybody* please read this word?"

"*Why!*" they shout.

The next word on the board is *how.*

"Please read this word."

"How," says the student.

"By looking at it and reading it," I say. "But if you want to, you can sound it out." Covering up the *ow,* I point to the *h.*

"What is this sound?"

"Hhh," says the student.

"Good." Covering up the *h* I point to the *ow.*

"What sound do these letters make?"

"Ow."

"Are you hurt?" I ask, looking concerned. "Are you OK?"

"Yes," says the student.

"Good. Then what sound do these letters make?"

"Ow."

"What's wrong? You keep saying 'ow.'"

"Nothing" is the usual reply.

"OK," I say, skeptically. "Now, please say this sound each time I touch these letters." I then point repeatedly to the letters *ow.*

"Ow, ow, ow, ow!"

I turn to the student next to him and say, "Are you doing anything to him? Are you poking him? Is that why he keeps saying 'ow'?"

The other student denies any wrongdoing.

"Everybody! What sound does this make?"

"*Ow!*"

I write the word *no* on the board. Yet another student is asked to read it.

"No."

"What do you mean, 'no'? Please read this word."

"No!"

I point out two or three other students in the class, asking each of them to read the word, and, of course, the response is always "No!" Again, the entire class is asked to read it, and I act quite annoyed at their response.

Finally, I write, *good-bye* on the board. I ask the entire class to read it.

"Good-bye!" they shout.

"What?" I ask.

"*Good-bye!*"

"OK, OK," I say. "I can take a hint. Good-bye." I start to walk out the door, waving as I do.

At this point, some of the students are saying, "Good-bye!" while others are shouting, "No! More!"

Throughout this "show" for the students, I would imitate Lou Costello's annoyed mannerisms and the irritated vocalizations he makes during his and "Bud" Abbott's legendary routine.

Of course, this is just an extension of the silliness that I use, but the responses from the children are usually great, and they all seem to enjoy it. On a couple of occasions, there have been some students who have literally fallen off of their chairs and rolled, doubled-up on the floor, laughing. I especially enjoyed doing these classroom performances when I was able to reach many students at one time (instead of just single students). In this process, I brightened the day for thirty students for a few minutes. I was able to give them some extra joy.

When I was working in different school buildings, I would do these routines perhaps a half dozen times at each building every year. The classroom teachers welcomed me back, year after year, to perform my routine with their subsequent classes. I really appreciated that.

As I approached retirement, I recognized that my ready-made audiences were going to disappear as soon as I walked out of those school doors for the last time. I wanted this practice—this mission—to continue, that someone, somewhere, would make a special effort to make a child's life a little better, a little more joyful, and a little less painful, through laughter.

Some very special colleagues and friends arranged for a retirement party for me when I left my last employment. At that gathering, I apologized to my fellow teachers for those little disruptions I had caused with the children over the years—when I was being silly—as they were trying to take their students back and forth in the halls in an orderly manner. It was also at that gathering that I explained what I was doing—that it was my goal to make a child laugh every day—and I explained why. I challenged them to try to do the same in their work, to make a special effort try to brighten a child's life just a little bit more, to give a child just an ounce of more joy than he or she would otherwise have.

Shortly after Erik died, I asked those around me (who knew and had contact with my son) to write something for me about Erik—share a bit about *their* interactions with him. I did this because I wanted to learn even more about him and to know what he meant to others. Many agreed to do this when I asked, but few followed through.

My father was one of those who did write a short note. He described a day during Erik's last summer when the two of them played together in the back yard of his house (my sister was babysitting him there that day). My father wrote that he played a little game in which he threw a rubber ball up onto the roof of the garage. My father said that—as the ball rolled off the roof—he positioned himself so that it would hit him on the head. He then acted startled and shouted, "Ouch!" He then threw the ball back onto the garage, repeating this process several times.

My father related that Erik apparently thought this was hilarious and laughed very loudly (and very much) every time the ball hit his grandfather's head. In fact, my father wrote that Erik laughed so hard that he became afraid that Erik "might hurt himself."

I'm sure that Erik was in no danger of harming himself because of all that laughter, and I am glad—for both of them—that Erik and his grandfather thoroughly enjoyed those minutes together. It made both of their lives just a little bit better; it enriched both of them.

Epilogue

We see our future as we wish it to be.
—Author

The old man was lying on a bed. The room had a vaguely familiar antiseptic smell to it.

He was at least aware of that much. He also knew that he had been in this bed for many days, perhaps weeks, but he wasn't exactly sure where he was or how he got there.

The old man did remember that he had had some visitors some time ago. He wasn't sure *when* they came, but he *did* remember that these special visitors were his dear children—all grown now.

Oh, he was so proud of them. They all had become successful in their own professions, all had married, and all were raising children of their own.

Children. He loved children, and he dearly loved his own children. The old man remembered when his children were born; each was so welcome and so wanted. He remembered when they were growing up that he would take care of them, play with them, and tuck them into bed with good-night kisses.

He had always told his little children that he loved them and cherished them. He hoped they knew that they knew they were very much wanted. He hoped that they remembered their childhoods pleasantly. He also remembered the years they had together, when he was their active father, interacting with them day to day. He enjoyed that. Although he was still their father, he was now in the background, more of an observer.

His adult children now had children of their own. It saddened him to know that—in their individual families—they, as parents, would come to experience many of the same troubles and problems that *he* had gone through when they were children in *his* family. The old man silently wished that he could spare his dear children from the pain and sorrows that they would certainly experience, but he knew that was impossible. Pain and sadness are integral parts of life, but so are happiness and joy. He hoped that his children would experience much more of the latter than the former. He hoped that life would be kinder—for them.

Just as his children were leaving his bedside, the old man tried to speak. He wondered if they were able to hear him. The effort was almost too much for him. He had moved his lips and whispered, "Know that I've always loved you…"

The old man now occasionally heard people talking in the distance, but it sounded like they were mumbling. He didn't know who they were or what they wanted. At times, someone would speak loudly, and it seemed like they were talking to him, but he still didn't understand what they were saying.

The old man concentrated on different sensations he was experiencing. One overriding impression was a general feeling of pain. He couldn't localize it to any specific place in his body; he just knew that it hurt. He also noted that this pain seemed to ebb and flow; occasionally, it would be a sharp, excruciating pain, and at other times it was a general, throbbing ache. But it was *always* there. Surprisingly, the old man didn't mind this agony—in fact, he almost welcomed it. The old man thought he *deserved* this pain. He hated himself. He knew that he was worthless and his life was worthless. It had *always* been so, and this pain was just part of what he deserved for just being alive. This agony was his penance for being who he was.

As he lay there, the old man also recognized that he was beginning to experience another sensation, one that was threatening to override his pain in its intensity. He was getting cold, *very* cold. This was not like the chill that one feels on a frosty day by having the furnace thermostat set too low or even being outside in the winter without a coat. This wasn't a coldness that he felt on his skin; this was a cold that he felt deep *inside*. This iciness appeared to emanate from the center of his body—from his very core. The cold he felt seemed to be threatening to overwhelm him. He didn't mind the pain as much as he hated this sense of being cold. He *detested* it!

The old man's mind drifted back to another time in his life when he had felt a coldness that reminded him of this sensation. It was when he was in his midteens, when he had gone deer hunting with his father and his two older brothers. After getting up very early and dressing warmly, they had all headed off for a two-hour drive into the mountains in search of their prey. Unfortunately, the heater in the car they were using was not working. *No matter,* he had thought. He was wearing warm clothes, and the outside temperature was sure to get warmer after the sun rose.

They reached their destination at daybreak and began their hunt, trekking up and down mountains and hillsides. Unfortunately, the sun didn't come out to warm him from his chilling early morning car ride. Instead, it snowed.

The snow had started lightly but steadily increased as the day wore on. This wasn't a light, powdery snow; it was a wet, large-flake snow.

The hunting group bore on, nevertheless, occasionally tracking deer footprints in the snow, winding their way deeper into the mountains. After a while, the new snow covered the tracks they were following, and the hunters went back to blindly trudging up and down hillsides. Only now, they were forcing their way through snow that was eight to ten inches deep and quickly getting deeper.

Throughout the day, the snow kept descending relentlessly on the group, sticking to their clothes. He remembered that his coat that day—well, *all* his clothes that day—were *not* waterproof. As the snowflakes accumulated on his coat, it melted and the moisture dissolved into the fabric. More snow dropped onto his clothes, and it melted too. Soon, his outer coat was soaked and the moisture spread to his sweater. The water from the constantly falling snow eventually drenched his coat, his sweater, shirt, undershirt, and finally reached his skin. As he trudged through the deep snow on the mountainside, the snow stuck to his pants and melted from the body heat emanating from his legs. The moisture permeated through his pants and through his long underwear, down through both pairs of socks, and again reached his skin.

After several hours of being assaulted by the icy weather in the mountains, their father decided that maybe they should go home, even though they were empty-handed. By the time they finally returned to their car, he remembered that he was completely and literally *soaked.*

As the two-hour ride back home began, he was quickly reminded that their car's heater was broken. Sitting in the front passenger seat, all he felt was cold air blowing on his legs during their entire return trip (his father had insisted on running the heater fan anyway, "in case the heater might start working." It didn't). The old man remembered that he had started to physically shiver during that return ride, and this shivering didn't stop.

After they reached their home, he went to his room to finally get out of his soaked clothes. It was difficult to unfasten his belt, the buttons, and the zippers with his cold-numbed fingers, and he struggled to take off each layer of clothing. His body shook uncontrollably during this process. When he finally worked his way out his denim pants, he noticed that the only place on all of his clothing that was *not* wet was a narrow strip of dry fabric around the top of his pants, where his belt had covered. *Everything* else was soaked. His shaking hands rubbed his body with dry towels. It literally took hours before he could stop shivering and begin to feel warmth inside him again.

That was cold, the old man remembered.

After experiencing the fading pain and the continually spreading iciness for what seemed to be an awfully long time, the old man began perceiving new sensations. The feeling of internal coldness slowly abated, and he noted that the ever-present pain seemed to be subsiding as well.

Unexpectedly, the old man began to feel warm. Just as the coldness seemed to emanate from his core, this warmth also came from the center of his being. As he lay there, relieved that the iciness had finally left him, he slowly became more aware of his surroundings. He sensed that there were people standing by his bed. He turned his head and gradually focused his eyes on his visitors. As they came into view, he saw two young people smiling at him.

He recognized them immediately.

"Pappa!" the little boy shouted excitedly, jumping up and down.

The old man slowly sat up and swung his legs off the side of the bed. Surprised at his new vitality, he reached down and scooped up the small boy in his arms. Tears poured down his aged, wrinkled face like a fresh stream of spring water over the cracked surface of a desert streambed. The old man hugged the little boy as he'd never hugged him before. He held his son tight; he could feel the warmth from the child's head on his face, and he recognized the familiar smell of his hair. His son hugged him back as well as he could, his little arms barely reaching around the old man's neck.

A teenage girl also stood there, smiling, watching her father and her brother reunite. She then leaned over and hugged them both, with her head resting on the old man's other cheek. He felt her silky hair on his face. He continued sobbing uncontrollably as he reached around to include his daughter within his protective arms.

After being locked together in this embrace for what seemed to be minutes, the girl stood up and looked directly into the old man's eyes.

"Don't cry, Pappa," she said, smiling. "We're here. We're together now. Everything's all right."

"Oh, yes! My beautiful children," the old man managed to blurt out between sobs, tears still flowing down his cheeks. "I've missed you *so* much!"

"We know, Pappa," she said tenderly. "We've missed you too. But now we're together, and we'll never be apart again."

With his hair wet from his father's tears, the small boy looked into the old man's red eyes and softly whispered, "No cry, Pappa. No cry," as he stroked the old man's wet, wrinkled cheek with his soft little hand.

After a few moments—as the old man was able to regain some of his composure—the girl pulled him by his hand, helping him to stand. He was still holding his son tight in his other arm.

The little boy reached up to him and took the old man's face in both of his small hands. He turned his father's face toward him and looked directly into the tired eyes. The child then said, "Go, Pappa. Go." But it wasn't the little boy who cried this time; it was the old man who wept anew, warm tears pouring down his face.

The girl reached around both her father and her brother, and hugged them again. These three were now joined together, connected in a renewed, perfect love for each other.

The old man felt overwhelmed; he recognized the long-lost sensation of *joy* slowly growing inside him, and he felt the very core of his being—his *center*—begin to tingle and glow. The feelings of love and attachment that had twice been ripped away from his soul returned, and the dark blanket that had suppressed the foundations of the old man's emotions for *so* long finally lifted.

That bond that he first felt in that hospital corridor so many decades past was restored, never to be broken again.

These three could now make up for lost time, to finally restore the years that had been stolen from them. Now, they had all the time in the world to be together.

Author Biography

Gunnar E. Skollingsberg, PhD, has lived through the tragic deaths of two of his children. A lifelong depression sufferer, Dr. Skollingsberg struggled to find the strength to carry on. Ultimately, he rallied around his love for his remaining children and a desire to bring comfort and laughter to lonely children everywhere.

Dr. Skollingsberg is a notable academic. He holds multiple degrees: two bachelor's degrees, a master's degree, and a doctorate in educational psychology. He has spent over twenty years as a public school teacher and twenty years as a school psychologist. His passion for education and mental-health awareness led him to focus his talents on making small, positive differences in kids' lives on a daily basis. This simple approach helps him deal with his ongoing pain and grief for his own lost children.

Dr. Skollingsberg is semi-retired and currently lives in Norway.

Made in the USA
Lexington, KY
21 February 2015